# Deliver This!

*Make the Childbirth Choice That's Right For You—*
*No Matter What Everyone Else Thinks*

## Marisa Cohen

Deliver This!
Make the Childbirth Choice That's Right For You—
No Matter What Everyone Else Thinks
Copyright ©2006 by Marisa Cohen

AVALON
publishing group incorporated

Published by
Seal Press
An Imprint of Avalon Publishing Group, Incorporated
1400 65th Street, Suite 250
Emeryville, CA 94608

ISBN-13: 978-1-58005-153-8
ISBN-10: 1-58005-153-7

Cohen, Marisa.
Deliver this!: make the childbirth choice that's right for you—no matter what everyone else thinks / Marisa Cohen.
p. cm.
ISBN-13: 978-1-58005-153-8
ISBN-10: 1-58005-153-7
1. Childbirth-Popular works. 2. Labor (Obstetrics)—Popular works. 3. Delivery (Obstetrics)—Popular works. I. Title.

RG525.C666 2006
618.4-dc22
        2006021115

Cover design by Gia Giasullo
Interior design by Stewart A. Williams
Printed in the United States of America by Malloy Lithography
Distributed by Publishers Group West

*Note: In some cases, names and identifying details have been changed to protect the privacy of the moms who generously shared their birth stories.*

For **BELLAMY** and **MOLLY**,

*who made 22.5 collective hours of labor worth every minute.*

# CONTENTS

# FROM PREGNANCY *to* MOTHERHOOD *in* ONE NOT-SO-SIMPLE STEP

I loved being pregnant. I really did. After I got past that initial phase when I felt constantly hungover and the only food I could choke down was lightly buttered sesame bagels, the next five or six months were pure bliss. I actually liked my new maternity clothes from Gap and Liz Lange better than my regular wardrobe, and I loved that complete strangers smiled at me and held the door as if I were a celebrity. I was also looking forward to having a baby in the house who I could cuddle and nurture and teach about baseball and Stephen Sondheim.

But I was in complete denial about the fact that to get from point A to point B, from pregnancy to parenthood, I would have to go through a completely life-altering, unimaginably intense moment of change called "childbirth." I could have told you everything you ever wanted to know about fertility cycles and cervical mucus, and every morning of my pregnancy I read about what my fetus was up to that day (cool, now she has nostrils!), but when it came to learning about that ultimate act of transition, the defining moment when I would go from pregnant woman to mom, I basically put my hands over my ears and screamed *"La la la la la, don't tell me, knock me out and wake me when it's over. . . ."*

Because up to that point, the only tales of childbirth I had come across—from my relatives, my friends in real life, my *Friends* on TV—involved vivid descriptions of excruciating pain. Think about how many times you have heard someone describe unbearable physical agony as "worse than child-birth." It tends to stick with you, no? Yeah, yeah, there's also the beauty of creating another human being and the miracle of nature and all that, but it was pretty hard to focus on the good stuff with all the images of sweat-drenched screaming women swirling through my head. I did have a few friends who had gone through natural childbirth, but whenever they rhapsodized about "good pain," my eyes glazed over and *Why, Why, WHY?* rang in my ears.

So whenever someone asked what my birth plan was, I just answered, "Drugs, lots of them." I never picked up a book about alternative pain-relief methods, and I never even did a single Google search on the topic (ironic, since I'll spend hours on the computer researching something way less significant, like finding the best Korean restaurant in Midtown).

Instead, from the moment I discovered I was pregnant, about six minutes after arriving home from a trip to Taiwan,

I automatically assumed I would go to the hospital, put myself in the hands of my skilled and capable doctors, and kick back with the epidural as soon as they let me. Natural childbirth, home birth, water birth—these were things that were not even in my field of reference. You might as well have said to me, "Hey, why not take a transporter beam to Borg Station 21 and give birth in a pool of ectoplasm?"

But even though I never put any real deliberation into where and how I was going to bring my baby into the world, I realize that I *had* made a decision by rejecting alternate methods and jumping right into the mainstream of American medicine. The question was, how did I get there?

If my life were a TV movie with those soft-focus flashbacks, and I had to pick one moment that set me on my inevitable path to a medicated hospital birth, I would go back to a gray Connecticut morning in the winter of 1986: After years of being woken up in the middle of the night with painful leg cramps (my pediatrician called them "growing pains," but even though I stopped growing at fourteen, the cramps remained), and getting pissed as hell at everyone's advice to just "stretch it out, walk it off, work through the pain," I visited my college health clinic, where the kindly doctor handed me some sample packets of a new pain reliever called Advil.

Cue the angels singing and the sun rising on a brand new day.

There it was, in that little white packet, instant relief from pains that had tormented me for as long as I could remember. From that moment on, I was never without an economy-size bottle of Advil in my medicine cabinet and a mini bottle in my backpack.

Over the following years, I tried several "natural" remedies for various problems, only to be disappointed each time. I popped some melatonin to prevent jet lag after a coworker swore up and down that it worked. It didn't work. I tried echinacea to prevent my annual winter sniffles after a friend swore it worked. It didn't work. All it did was convince me that herbal supplements should be lumped in the same money-sucking-scam category as those phony emails saying that the deposed prince of Rwanda wants to share his unclaimed bank account with you.

I occasionally tried New Agey disciplines like yoga and meditation, and I liked them well enough as relaxation and exercise, but I was highly skeptical of their ability to really help out when the going got tough. A deep, cleansing breath or a soothing child pose had nothing on my beloved bottle of ibuprofen.

So all right, it's a given that I was predisposed to medicated birth over the natural method. But even if I had the inclination to consider other methods, when would I have had the time to do anything about it? Planning a natural birth takes research, classes, practice. Planning a hospital birth is easy—you just show up and the medical staff does the rest. Even with my company's fairly generous maternity-leave policy, I knew that any days I took off before giving birth would come out of the number of days I would get *after* the baby was here, so I literally worked up to the minute I went into labor (though I didn't realize until after the fact that those annoying back pains during the staff meeting were early contractions).

The months leading up to the birth were a frenzy of getting my act together: making sure all my assignments were done, filling out medical forms, figuring out where the baby would sleep in our small apartment, stocking up on wipes, diapers, bibs, onesies, and thermometers, and then hiding them from my suddenly superstitious mother.

With so many other decisions to make (like what on earth should we name this kid?—after opting to find out we were having a girl—and what kind of childcare could we afford?), it was kind of a relief not to have to think about the details of actually giving birth. We had dutifully taken a "Preparing for Childbirth" class at the hospital, but that was more about watching videos, learning how to diaper a plastic doll, and socializing with the other couples. A friend of mine, who had given birth to both her girls in a birthing-center bathtub without any drugs, urged me to write out a detailed birth plan before I left for the delivery room, but I brushed her off. I truly felt that once those hospital doors swung shut behind me, I was in the hands of the pros and they would know what to do.

So here's how it went: On a warm Wednesday night in July 2001, after being cranky, whiny, and uncomfortable all day at work, I felt a *pop* in my stomach just as my husband, my best friend, and I were finishing dinner at an

Italian restaurant down the block. As I started down the steps of the restaurant, I felt something oily streaming down my leg. "Don't panic," I whispered to my husband Jeremy, "but I think my water just broke." We went home to call my doctor and get my overnight bag, and even though I was nervous and had no idea what to expect, I started giggling uncontrollably with excitement as we hailed a cab to the hospital.

A nurse or a resident (I can't remember which; they all seemed way too young to be allowed to practice medicine) confirmed that my water had indeed broken and paged the doctor on call, who suggested I start walking laps around the delivery-ward corridor to get the labor going. *This isn't so bad,* I thought as I hobbled around and joked with the nurses who were on the night shift. But within minutes, I wasn't joking anymore. First I threw up my fettuccine bolognese, and then I sat on the toilet while everything else came out the other end. By then I was in immense pain, but I was dilated less than two centimeters, and the doctor, who had finally arrived to check on me, told me she wouldn't give me an epidural until I was at four. I couldn't walk around the halls anymore—not because of any hospital rules, but because each step made me double over in agony.

For the next couple of hours, all I could do was sit up cross-legged on the end of my hospital bed in complete silence and darkness (any sensory stimulation at this point was excruciating) and wait for the contractions, which felt like a million tiny hands grabbing every vein and piece of skin and muscle around my back and waist and squeezing as tightly as possible. When Jeremy tried to rub my back, I told him in no uncertain terms to get his hands off me. The only relief I got was from taking a deep breath and then blowing out as hard as I could.

At some point, after I begged the doctor to do something for the pain, she started me on Stadol, a painkiller administered through my IV line that she said would "take the edge off." That's when I started hallucinating: Between contractions I saw little unicorns floating around the room on top of giant gumballs. That distracted me for a good couple of minutes, but as soon as the contractions came, the happy little unicorns evaporated and I was jolted back into reality. Finally, the doctor checked me again around 5:00 AM and announced that I was three and a half centimeters, close enough for the epidural.

Once the epidural kicked in (which, by the way, was far less traumatic than getting a flu shot), I was happy as a kitten. I could finally unclench my muscles, relax for a bit, do the crossword puzzle, call my parents. But while I calmed down, my labor decided to take a breather, too. I was like a car stuck in the mud, refusing to go past four centimeters, so my doctor started me on Pitocin, a synthetic form of the hormone oxytocin, to kick my labor into action.

For the next fourteen hours, I had the following items attached to me: an IV, an epidural catheter, a urinary catheter, a bloodpressure cuff that automatically squeezed my arm every fifteen minutes (making napping impossible), the fetal monitor, and, for a little while, an oxygen mask. I was basically a pregnant pincushion. I couldn't get up, I wasn't allowed to eat, and I had to pee through a tube I couldn't even feel. Not that I was complaining. At that point I was so happy to be relieved of the pain that I truly didn't care how many tubes were poking out of me.

Throughout my twenty-one hours of labor, I saw a succession of people: many lovely, helpful nurses (including a student, who told me as she inserted my catheter that it was her first time ever, putting me in the weird position of talking her through it while silently praying she wouldn't screw it up). Each of the three doctors in my OB's practice checked in on me at some point. I was thrilled, though, that when it was finally time to push, my main doctor was on duty (whichever doc happens to be on call when you are ready to push gets to do the honors). She was a warmly intelligent woman my own age, and we spent half the time at my checkups joking around, but when push literally came to shove, she seemed larger than life and completely in charge.

Even though the first part of labor took almost an entire day, I managed to push out my barely six-pound daughter in less than thirty minutes. My doctor showed her to me, then handed her off to a couple of pediatric residents, who fussed over her in the plastic bassinet next to my bed, suctioning, weighing, measuring, eye-dropping. I kept asking my husband, "What does she look like? Is she blond or brunette?" In what afterward seemed like an eternity later, but was probably only three or four minutes, she was handed to me. I stared at her: She was red-faced, with wet blond hair and little rolls of skin peeling off her tiny hands, and there was something in her face that reminded me of my father. I was suddenly a mother. I'd mainly been a passenger on the ship that transported me from the state of blissful pregnancy to the new world of dazed parenthood, but Bellamy and I were both healthy, my long labor had come to a satisfying conclusion, and that was all that mattered to me.

That was the end of one story, but the beginning of another. In the course of those twenty-one hours of clenching, dozing, breathing, hallucinating, and pushing, my life completely and irrevocably changed. I knew that having a baby would transform almost everything, from how many hours I slept to the way I related to my own parents, but what took me by surprise was the way I started thinking about childbirth, and the way that having gone through it connected me in a visceral way to every other mother I encountered.

After being in denial for so long, it was like a dam broke, and all of a sudden I couldn't stop talking about childbirth. Everywhere I went, I ran into dazed women who collectively felt the need to spill every detail about their own experience—the good, the bad, the ugly, and the amazing. Any modesty we had before flew out the window. I found myself standing in line at the supermarket discussing episiotomies and vaginal tears with a woman I'd never met before—but she had a newborn and I had a newborn, so we were instantly soul mates. I sat in new-mom support groups and Kindermusic classes, listening to other women recount their birth stories, and then I would share mine, refining the details each time. Each morning I logged on to a message board for mothers of July 2001 babies, where women posted long accounts of their tours of duty in the delivery room. We were like those war veterans who gather at the VA hall to share their battle stories with the only other people who really understand.

But as warm and cathartic as this new-mom bonding ritual was on the surface, I soon started to notice an unpleasant sense of tension and criticism bubbling just underneath. I saw eyes start to roll when a mom nursing a baby in a sling talked about squatting in a bathtub while her doula rubbed her back. I had one friend confess to me that she'd stopped telling people how happy she was with her C-section because of all the thinly veiled reactions of horror she got. I realized that while we were not shy at all about sharing the most intimate details of childbirth, we backed off from discussing *why* we made these decisions, afraid of offending, or being offended by, someone who didn't agree with us. This influx of information without the context led to a whole lot of misunderstanding and judgment.

And, I hate to admit, I was just as guilty of this as anyone else. I joined in the chorus of medicated-childbirth moms who questioned why anyone would be a martyr and choose to go through such an excruciating ordeal without drugs. "You wouldn't have a root canal without drugs," I said more than once, "so how is this any different?" I nodded in agreement as other friends said, "She must think she's a better mother because she suffered for her child."

At the same time, I heard natural-childbirth advocates describe a hospital birth—especially a C-section—as "such an incredibly sad way to have a child." While some of the women I knew were disappointed and even, yes, depressed that they wound up under the knife, other women were secretly relieved, and there were a few who say they can't imagine why anyone would undergo the pain and unpredictability of vaginal childbirth when a safe surgical option exists. These women were pissed as hell that anyone would dare judge them for their choice or tell them that one of the happiest moments of their lives was "sad and unfortunate." Isn't this what all that marching in the '70s was about? We fought for the right to take control of our bodies, so why on earth should anyone question how another woman chooses to handle the most profound event her body might ever experience?

And of course, I couldn't ponder all this without wondering how my own state of denial and unwillingness to even consider other options affected my own birth experiences. If I had actually pushed aside my fear and read some straightforward information about other birthing methods, would I have incorporated any of it into my own birth plan? I know I would have still eventually asked for the drugs, but if I had waited a little longer before rushing to the hospital and tried some other pain management methods at home, would my labor have moved faster, requiring less intervention? Would I have actually made a birth plan? If I hadn't had any drugs, would that moment when they handed the baby to me *really* have been as magical as the websites, magazines, and TV shows claim? Does who you are as a person dictate how you choose to give birth, and does that in turn change the way you are as a parent?

But most of all, I wondered, at a time when we are all stressed out, sleepless, and trying to find steady footing on that wobbly middle ground between self and mom, why are we making each other feel worse?

In my quest to find out what it is that leads women down the path to giving birth in a hospital, birthing center, or even in a plastic kiddie pool parked on their living room floor—and why we all feel so invested in everyone else's choice—I have spoken to midwives and doctors, I've read medical journals and blogs, but most of all, I have talked to moms. Over the course of several eye-opening, mind-blowing months, I listened as more than one hundred mothers talked about their birth experiences, how they got there, and what the aftermath was.

And you know what? Not one of them was crazy. There were no martyrs in the group, and no one who thought her birth should be conveniently planned around her ski vacation. Every single woman had a compelling explanation of why her birth choice was the best one for her. Not all of them wound up having the experience they dreamed of—and I'll talk about that, too. But every single one of them wanted me to know that at the time, they thought they were making the healthiest and safest choice for them and their child.

Of course, the question of "safest" and "healthiest" is

not at all cut-and-dried. In my experience as a health writer, I have found that no matter what your opinion is on a health issue, somehow, somewhere, there is a published study to back you up (it may have been done on a dozen subjects in a small town in Sweden, but still, it's there and you can quote it). And I've also found that if a medical journal swears something is true this month, next month someone else will prove exactly the opposite.

I am not here to make any judgments about which birth option is best, because only you can decide which is the right choice for you. This book is intended to be a judgment-free forum where women can openly discuss one of the most deeply personal and emotional decisions of their lives.

Whether you're pregnant now or hope to be sometime in the future, I hope this book will help you cut through all the background noise and get an honest, all-inclusive overview of the options available to you in early twenty-first-century America. If you've been through labor and are bewildered by your own experience, or by the reactions and criticisms of others, I hope this book will give you some insight and comfort (or if you read it and still swear you would do everything exactly the same the next time, then I'm thrilled that I confired how perfect your choice was for you).

But most of all, I want this book to take some of the pressure off us all. There are so many *other* people who are going to judge what we do (the media, our bosses, our mothers) that we really should have each other's backs. Let's make a pact to say, *Hey, you went through thirty-four hours of labor without even taking a Tylenol for the pain? Mazel tov! What a lovely baby. You had a scheduled C-section and never even felt one contraction? Way to go, what a beautiful baby. You thought you were going to have a home birth but had complications and had to be rushed to the hospital? Sorry it didn't work out as you planned, but hey, what an adorable baby.*

## CHAPTER ONE

# THE FIRST SHOT FIRED *in the* MOMMY WARS

For the first three or four weeks after my husband and I discovered I was pregnant, we told no one—not even our parents or best friends. It was our delicious little secret. We knew there would be plenty of important decisions to make soon enough about things like breastfeeding and my post-baby career plans, and we knew there would be no shortage of people eager to jump right in and share their opinions about those choices. But for those few weeks, it was just the two of us, our little peanut, and a world of possibilities.

Looking back, that was a truly idyllic time. Because as soon as I let the world in on my secret and stepped up to accept my public role as Pregnant Woman, everyone—from my family to my coworkers to the boundary-deficient older women on the street who stopped to pat my belly—had something to say about what was the best way to have a baby and be a mom. And as much as I tried to keep my focus steady on what made the most sense for my little family, I realized that, like it or not, I was soon going to be thrust belly-first into the Mommy Wars.

You're probably sick of hearing that phrase—*Mommy Wars*. Me, too. Half the time I'm convinced the media has picked it as the controversy du jour and blown it way out of proportion; the rest of the time I'm convinced it's absolutely true. Books, magazines, and chat-show hosts constantly remind us about the ongoing battle between stay-at-home moms and working moms, breastfeeders and formula fans. And those are just two of the most high-profile talking points: It seems that *every* decision you make about raising a child in the twenty-first century, no matter how personal, is going to push someone else's buttons. Daycare or nanny? City or suburbs? Public school, private school, or home school? Vaccinate or not? Ban Barbies or let your daughter revel in all her plastic-princess glory? (For me, these pressures all came to a head a couple of years later, when I found myself at the playground, hovering over my crying child; she had just scraped her chin, and I was paralyzed with embarrassment after offering her an Elmo Band-Aid in front of another mother who I knew tried to avoid any pop-cultural influence in her kid's life. It was a just a freakin' Band-Aid, and yet I felt as if I were making a statement about my core philosophies of child rearing in America.)

Well, whatever is driving the Mommy Wars—the media or moms themselves—one fact is unavoidable: The battles begin before you even have the baby.

More than four million women give birth in the United States every year,[1] which means there are roughly forty billion opinions on how to do it best. It may be your body and your baby, but how you choose to deliver that child seems to be everybody else's concern. To get an idea of the kind of tension surrounding the issue of childbirth choices, try walking into a maternity store filled with women trying on stretch-panel jeans and nursing bras, and say loudly enough for everyone to hear, "So, I'm really excited about doing a home birth. We're renting a birthing pool, and my husband is planning on catching the baby!" People will stop dead in their tracks—sure, a few might be fascinated and encouraging, but most will be absolutely shocked. As they pretend to sort through that pile of oversize T-shirts, they'll raise their eyebrows and whisper loud enough for you to hear, "Is she crazy? Who would do such a thing?"

Or go on a message board for moms-to-be and type in a question like this: "What do you think about scheduling an elective C-section? I really don't see the need to go through vaginal childbirth when there is a perfectly safe alternative." Then sit back and enjoy the fireworks, as the moms who support C-section-by-choice trade nasty messages with those who see the procedure as nothing more than a selfish cop-out.

Even the most mainstream birth option, attempting vaginal delivery in a hospital, has its share of potential landmines. Should you attempt to labor as drugfree as possible, letting your body function as nature designed? Or does that mean needlessly suffering unbearable pain? Is artificial labor induction a lifesaving (and time-saving) tool, or is it just going to lead to a cascade of other intrusive interventions? Is it more prudent to deliver with an obstetrician who is trained for medical emergencies, or with a midwife who will provide more personal, less invasive care?

When I was at a dinner party recently, I sat across from a woman who was seven months pregnant. She was glowing, not just from her impending motherhood, but with excitement about the intensive natural-birth class she was taking. She was planning on delivering at a major hospital that offered every high-tech intervention, but she hoped to avoid an epidural and all its attendant baggage (catheters, fetal monitors) by learning how to use relaxation techniques to control the pain. The woman sitting on the other side of me kicked me under the table and muttered under her breath, "Jeez, just get the epidural. What's the big deal?" The very idea of attempting an unmedicated birth is seen by many women as a radical and masochistic endeavor. Meanwhile, the idea of a hooked-up, numbed-down, doctor-driven birth is viewed by many natural-birth moms as paternalistic, depressing, and ultimately more dangerous than laboring naturally.

While this frenzy of opinions can make your head spin as you try to sort out who is right and what is safest, it's important to remember that it's all a by-product of the fact that we *do* have such a range of birth options today. If you have a healthy pregnancy and an uncomplicated labor, and you are willing to put in the research time and preparation, you can opt to try for as high-tech or low-tech a birth as you wish. And if someone disagrees with your choice, well, it's none of their business, is it?

But that's the frustrating thing. People really do believe it *is* their business. Your family members, especially, will take your decisions about childbirth very personally. It may be your baby, but it's their granddaughter, niece, or godson, and they believe they have every right to say how that child should enter the world. When you got that lip ring or decided to switch your major from accounting to Renaissance lit, they may not have been thrilled, but hey, it's your life. This decision, however, is going to affect the next link in the family chain, so they will worry, they will question your decisions, and they will nudge you to do what they believe is best—even if their beliefs are based on the latest scientific breakthroughs of 1962.

At least your family has an excuse—it's their job to be in your face. But what about those women in the maternity store, or those complete strangers typing angrily at you online? Why is it that people who have absolutely no personal investment in your child can have such a strong opinion about your plans on how to deliver it?

It all begins with that very admirable human instinct to throw a protective arm around an innocent baby, no matter whose baby it is. Even though, at the click of a mouse, there is an overload of information about every type of childbirth available, most of us tend only to read up on the option we have already chosen. Without any solid information, many women's first reaction when they hear about a different type of birth experience is that it can't possibly be safe—and what caring person wouldn't show concern for the health and well-being of a helpless little baby? When you truly believe, as the majority of women in this country do, that a hospital birth is the Cadillac of options, the shining result of a century of scientific research and medical advances, then it can be rather alarming to hear a mom-to-be announce that she is opting out. At the same time, if you truly believe, as a smaller but still significant number of women do, that hospitals are inherently dangerous places, responsible for far too many unnecessary interventions, then it can be mind-boggling to think that most American women choose to deliver there without considering the alternatives.

But what starts as an understandable sense of concern for the baby can easily blend into contempt for the mother. *How could she make such a choice? This is not just about her body—it's about her baby's life.* And that's when we start blaming each other for that huge, unforgivable sin of motherhood: placing our own needs above those of our babies.

And that, dear readers, is what every battle in the Mommy Wars is really all about. Whether you are arguing about working or staying at home, breastfeeding, co-sleeping, or the wisdom of trying to toilet-train a six-month-old, the heart of the matter is this: What is best for the baby, and what is best for the mom? And if those two answers are incompatible, who wins? Are the best interests of the mom also inherently the best for the baby, since they result in a happier, more fulfilled parent who can take better care of her child? Or are the baby's needs so formative and crucial in those first few years that they take precedence over everything else? And who makes the final determination of what is best for *any* baby? Do you listen to your pediatrician, your mother, Dr. Spock, Dr. Sears, other women? Or do you tune them all out and just listen to your own instincts? All those questions are right there in that very first maternal decision about where and how to give birth.

Some women, particularly those who make so-called radical childbirth choices, will get a pretty strong preview of the Mommy Wars as soon as they verbalize their decision. But let's face it, the rest of us are probably not thinking about the greater social context of childbirth when we make our choices: We are simply thinking about our bodies and our babies. And the most visceral reason we go on the offensive when we hear about other women's choices is that it is an instinctive way of defending our *own* choices. *If you say that your decision about how to deliver a baby is the right one, then you must be saying that mine is wrong.* No one wants to feel that her experience is somehow second-best. We want to believe that we are doing what makes the most sense. We want to believe that we are giving our babies the healthiest and safest entries into the world, and that we are setting the scene for the warmest, most loving introduction of mother to baby.

Those feelings are perfectly normal, and evolutionarily necessary—they're one of the first signs of that fierce lioness protectiveness that nature thoughtfully provides us with. But why does there have to be only one "best" way? Just as everyone's bodies, backgrounds, and beliefs are different, what is "safe," "best," and "right" can be completely different from one Mama Lion to the next. Think how liberating it will be if we collectively get to a point where we can see our own childbirth choices as something distinct and unconnected to anyone else's, where we can be absolutely content in our choices and absolutely respectful of everyone else's.

This is all very easy for me to say now, but I will be the first to admit that it took me a while to achieve this "birth and let birth" attitude. It didn't come in one perfect "aha" moment when I sat up in bed, slapped my forehead, and realized that delivering in a birth center was as safe and legitimate an option for my friend as delivering in a hospital was for me. It came after two or three years of being immersed in the diverse, opinionated, sometimes frustrating, but ultimately wonderful world of moms.

When Bellamy was born and I left the land of cubicles and expense-account lunches to become a freelance writer,

## More Moms Are Waiting

Moms are older and wiser, and they know what they want: The average age of a first-time mother in the United States was 25.2 in 2003, an all-time high. Birth rates for women under 24 have been on the decline since 1990, while birth rates for women over 35 keep going up, and the birth rate for women in their early forties has grown by an astounding 58 percent over the last decade and a half.[2]

my social life entered a new phase, with a brand-new cast of characters. Before, all my closest friends had either gone to high school or college with me, or had worked on the editorial staff at one of the half-dozen magazines I'd passed through in my career. In other words, we had a lot in common, from our backgrounds to our educations to our politics. And we all had pretty similar ideas about childbirth. In fact, a couple of my friends even shared the same obstetrician and delivered at the same hospital as me. So there was no reason to ever question my belief that a medicated hospital birth was the best possible way to go.

But then I became a mom, and things changed. My old friends who had babies lived too far away to hang out with on a daily basis; the friends who lived nearby were still single. And one fact that all new moms quickly discover is that no matter how much your friends love you and no matter how delighted they are with your adorable new child, if they don't have babies of their own, they are going to have a very limited capacity to listen to you fret about clogged milk ducts or the color of your baby's poop. My solution to this, after spending a couple of months hanging out almost exclusively with a baby who was very sweet but not the world's greatest conversationalist, was to meet other new moms. Frankly, I didn't care if we had anything more in common than location and babies. If they were nice, if they could talk about movies and midnight feedings without missing a beat, I wanted to be their friend. I discovered UrbanBaby.com— the Match.com of the peewee set (*4-mo.-old girl in Village seeks same for swinging in Washington Sq. Pk.*)—and within months I had made a dozen or so new friends.

While some of the women I met would have fit right in with my old gang, there were others who traveled in completely different pre-baby worlds. My newly formed playgroup included a nurse, a fashion designer, a lawyer, and a stay-at-home mom who had recently moved to New York from a rambling farmhouse in rural Pennsylvania. There were moms from large, conservative families and from small, liberal ones; from the Philippines, New England, old England, and the Midwest. Our ages ranged from late twenties to mid-forties; our living situations ranged from barely getting by to obscenely wealthy (in New York City, these two extremes can exist within blocks of each other).

And as diverse as our backgrounds and lifestyles were, so were our birth stories. On any given afternoon, I could be sitting on a park bench with one mom who delivered in a birth center, another who chose to induce, a third who had an elective C-section, and a fourth who adopted. And yes, when we shared these stories for the first time—sometimes within moments after we met—I felt the tension, the eye rolling, the silent judgment underneath the smiles. But instead of really discussing our feelings about childbirth, we moved on to more pressing and less divisive issues, like how to deal with various post-baby issues in our marriages and where to buy the best children's shoes in lower Manhattan.

Over time, as our babies grew, we all grew closer. My mom friends not only helped me pass those otherwise excruciating hours between naptime and dinnertime, but they became a crucial support system during all those bumps in the road of motherhood. I found myself emailing or talking to some of them every day. No one else but another mom could possibly have understood the mania surrounding preschool applications or potty training.

And then we all started having babies again. Boom, boom, boom, one after another, several tiny new playgroup members were born in a span of just a few months. I found that this time, when I heard about a natural birth or an elective C-section, I was more curious than dismissive. *Well,* I thought, *if that mom is as cool and funny and smart as I think she is, then there must be an interesting reason why she made that choice.* So I tentatively started asking questions: Why did this method of childbirth seem so right for you? How did you prepare for it? Were you worried about what would happen if something went wrong? How did you cope with the most arduous parts of labor? Did your family support your decision? Was the experience everything you had hoped it would be? And when I heard the answers, I found that almost everything I had assumed about why women shun drugs or choose surgery was pretty much dead wrong. As I talked to more and more women, I became fairly obsessed with the topic. I discovered that a birth choice is not just about delivering a baby; it is about everything in your life that has led you to that moment. And the great thing is, when you go ahead and ask, women *love* to tell you their answers. I have yet to come across a mom who didn't have a strong opinion one way or the other and her own compelling story to go with it.

And the great thing is that once you begin to understand how such a deeply personal choice as how to deliver your baby is made, it becomes that much easier to have a more balanced view of other debates in the Mommy Wars. Instead of just holding on to your first reaction when you hear about a mom who is making very different choices about childrearing from your own, you can pull back and see the larger picture, how her background, beliefs, and circumstances have led her to a very different place on the vast spectrum of motherhood choices—one that makes as much sense for her as yours does for you. So just as the Mommy Wars begin with the battle over childbirth choices, maybe the Mommy Truce can start there, too.

## CHAPTER TWO

# ALL ABOUT CONTROL: TAKING CHARGE *vs.* LETTING GO

From the moment I felt that fluid oozing down my leg on the stairs of the Italian restaurant, I became aware of one indisputable fact of childbirth: You have absolutely no control over the situation. Unlike, say, peeing in your pants, when you can try to squeeze yourself to a stop, when your water breaks you can't do anything about it. You just have to wait till it's over, then grab some paper towels and smile while you pray the waiter doesn't skid on the mess and dump a lasagna in someone's lap.

Up until that point, I had been used to being in control. I had managed the copy desks at major magazines, making schedules and keeping on top of the flow of pages through the different departments. I had overseen work on my apartment, which involved giving directions to crews of workers who spoke three different languages. Even with my pregnancy, I micromanaged just how much information was doled out to relatives and friends and planned every detail of my maternity leave (which, by the way, was shot to hell when I went into labor eleven days before my due date, screwing up my exit strategy and making me miss my office baby shower).

I had even come up with a plan for how my labor would begin. I would take a week off from work, giving me time to get one of those rose-petal pedicures I had read about, see a bunch of movies, and do any last-minute shopping for baby gear. Then, one evening while Jeremy was lovingly reading the latest Harry Potter book to my belly, the contractions would start—soft, gentle waves that I could breathe through easily for a few hours. We would go out for a walk, perhaps get some ice cream. We would then casually head to the hospital, where Jeremy would massage my back with tennis balls until it was time to get the epidural. (My reverie ended there. The actual birth of the baby was beyond my contemplation.)

But then reality got in the way. When my daughter picked her own inconvenient time and place to start her journey, I could do nothing more than go along for the ride. I could control how the labor played out about as well as I could control the peace process in the Middle East. Two years later, when I gave birth to my second daughter, Molly, I went in with some idea of what to expect, but I still had that same panicked feeling of losing control, and the labor went so quickly that I didn't have a chance to even contemplate following a birth plan or controlling the pain. I just grabbed the doctor by his scrubs as my baby practically flew out of me.

Among the many things that are out of your control during childbirth are when and where your labor starts. You can't control what position the baby is in and whether or not she wants to come out. You certainly can't control what sounds you are going to make and what obscenities you might scream out in the middle of all of it. One of the big secrets of childbirth that we all tend to talk about only *after* the fact is that you can't control your bodily functions, either: You are going to vomit, and you are very likely going to poop in front of other people (when you start pushing, everything down there comes out). You can't control whether any other complications with the baby or with your own health will get in the way of your ideal birth scenario.

A complete loss of control over your own body is horrifying to some women and liberating to others, and the way you respond to that concept is one of the primary forces that informs your birth choice. Midwives I talked to spoke of "getting out of the way of your body," and "letting go of the idea that you can control childbirth." Many of the natural-birth mothers I interviewed admitted that they didn't truly begin to get in sync with their labor until they gave in to the fact that they could not control it or even, in some cases, control the pain, despite what they learned in childbirth classes. "The first hour, I didn't know what I was doing or what position I should be in," said Beth, who gave birth to her second child at home after a disappointing hospital experience the first time. "In my mind, I was thinking I had to control it. But when I realized that I just had to let it happen. I was able to relax, and he came right out. It was the easiest birth."

Give in and let your body do what it was designed by nature to do best—that's one school of thought. But don't tell that to all the scientists and doctors who have worked so hard over the last century to find ways to tame this wild animal called "childbirth." By using drugs to induce labor or stop premature contractions, doctors have been trying to nail down the timing of labor to that optimal forty-week window when the baby is fully cooked but not so large as to get stuck on the way out. Scheduled C-sections can bypass the unpredictable process of labor altogether. The development of anesthetics—from chloroform (first used in a delivery in 1847, it hit the big time in 1853 when Queen Victoria declared it "delightful beyond measure"),[1] to morphine–based "twilight sleep" in the first half of the twentieth century, to nitrous oxide, Demerol, and epidurals—has been a continuing effort to give women control over the pain of labor. Some natural-birth advocates argue that early treatments were developed to give medical practitioners a sense of control over their otherwise screaming patients, which may be partly true, but records show that most doctors initially resisted using the treatments because it was difficult to gauge a safe dosage, and because it was harder to deliver a baby from a narcotized woman who couldn't push effectively.[2]

For many of the women I interviewed, taking advantage

of these pain-control methods is the logical way to reestablish order in the midst of chaos. "To this day, I have no idea why people don't ask for pain medicine," said Sharon, a mom of two in St. Louis. "I enjoyed the birth of my children so much because I was comfortable. I felt that *I* was in control of the situation, instead of having the pain control me."

In fact, the historian Edward Shorter has noted that developments such as birth control, anesthesia, and standardized C-sections were giving women more power over their reproductive lives than ever before. "By 1930, the technical means existed for letting the mother herself control every aspect of the birth process," he writes.[3] Yet, he says, that full sense of control never really happened. Once we got to a point where women didn't have to worry so much about dying in childbirth or catching childbed fever (often caused by unsanitary conditions, such as doctors who went straight from the morgue to the delivery room without so much as rinsing their hands, this infection of the reproductive system was one of the leading causes of maternal death from both childbirth and abortions up to the 1940s),[4] doctors turned their focus away from the mother and toward the baby, making sure it had what they believed was the easiest, safest, and least stressful journey into the world. Control in the delivery room was put firmly in the hands of the doctor, who routinely turned to interventions such as episiotomies (cutting the tissue between the vagina and anus to allow more room for the baby's head to emerge) and C-sections to get the baby out as quickly as possible. In fact, in the very first issue of the

*American Journal of Obstetrics & Gynecology,* published in 1920, the renowned physician Joseph B. DeLee argued that virtually all childbirth is pathologic, and that sedation, episiotomy, and forceps should be used in every case.[5]

As I read more and more about early childbirth practices, it became very clear that the entire history of childbirth has been about control. Over the years, power has shifted from women to men, from midwives to physicians, from patients to practitioners, and now, in many cases, right back to the mothers themselves. From the time humans first walked upright to the early nineteenth century, childbirth was primarily a women-only club. Sure, men had a part in getting the process started, but once labor began, moms, mothers-in-law, grandmothers, aunts, and, most important, female midwives, took charge, guiding the mother through the process.

Men first started pressing their way into the birthing room in the eighteenth century, when male midwives became fashionable accessories for upper-class women—sort of like today's trend of having a Bugaboo stroller or a British nanny. But it wasn't until the early nineteenth century that women of means started switching over to male doctors (these were general practitioners—obstetrics didn't become a specialty until the 1900s). But still, whether attended by a rural midwife or a university-trained physician, the vast majority of births took place at home.[6]

Then, in the early twentieth century, one of the biggest battles for control took place, between traditional midwives at home and male doctors in hospitals. Until then, hospitals were considered grimy, dark, depressing—a last resort to be used only by poor and unwed mothers. That started to change in the 1920s and 1930s, when doctors started to learn more about infection and took more precautions against the spread of germs. Women began to realize that C-sections were occasionally necessary, and that they could best be performed in hospitals. Families began to move around, so women didn't necessarily have that ready–made female support group to surround them during birth. Private rooms for patients who could afford them changed the public image of hospitals from scary houses of illness to clean, comfortable sanctuaries.

## Has Childbirth Really Gotten Safer?

At the turn of the twentieth century, for every one thousand women who gave birth in the United States, six to nine died of pregnancy-related complications, most of those due to infection caused by unsanitary conditions or botched interventions.[8] At the turn of the twenty-first century, the maternal death rate had dropped to 1.2 per ten thousand births.[9] However, this is still almost *double* the rates of most European nations, Canada, and Australia.[10]

As a result of this shift, midwives were suddenly looked upon as remnants of the pre-industrialized world—a view that was certainly encouraged by physicians, who were in direct competition with their services. Much like the corner coffee shop being pushed out by the ubiquitous Starbucks, midwives began to be phased out. In 1901, midwives attended half of all American births; by the 1970s, that number was less than 1 percent.[7]

While it is very clear that the demand for anesthetics and baby-saving technologies—and therefore hospital birth— was driven by women themselves, who welcomed relief from the pain that had generally been accepted as "God's punishment for women,"[11] some childbirth historians argue that the movement from home to hospital was spurred primarily by doctors, who wanted to transport the patient from her home turf to theirs. At home, she was still the queen of the castle, with scads of relatives chirping around, peering over the doctor's shoulder and critiquing his work. By bringing the patient into his domain, the doctor could exert both medical and emotional control.

In any case, an intertwined combination of doctor's prerogative and patient's desire rapidly altered the childbirth landscape. In 1920, only 21 percent of births took place in the hospital; by 1955, it was 94 percent.[12] By the time we hit the 1960s, virtually all births in America (except for those occuring within religious groups that held firm to tradition) had become medicalized and entirely controlled by doctors. You checked into the hospital and dutifully obeyed orders. As my mother has often told me about giving birth in the late 1960s, "The doctors told your father to go see a movie, then they knocked me out, and when I woke up, they handed me a baby."

This type of birth, in which the mother had little say in her own care, may have been accepted by most as a small price to pay for a safe, pain-free birth, but there were rumblings of discontent. And those noises only grew louder as women talked and met and marched and realized there might be a better, more fulfilling way to give birth. In the age of "I Am Woman, Hear Me Roar" and *Our Bodies, Ourselves,* women were fighting for free love, birth control, and abortion rights, so why should they abdicate control over their bodies when they gave birth? The growing popularity of the Lamaze method and books such as Dr. Grantley Dick-Read's *Childbirth Without Fear* helped propel a movement toward more natural, mom-friendly methods of birth. In 1975, a group of women in New York City brainstormed ideas for the ideal gentle birth experience and created the Childbearing Center, the country's first out-of-hospital, family-centered, Board of Health–approved place to give birth. Midwives started growing in popularity again, and by the turn of the twenty-first century, they were attending 8 percent of U.S. births.[13]

So here we are. There are new technologies being developed every day to gain more control over birth: more sophisticated ultrasounds, advanced prenatal screenings, walking epidurals. A middle-class woman giving birth in America can choose to deliver her baby in the most high-tech, computer-aided, medicalized way possible, or she can choose to bring her baby into the world the same way her ancestors did: at home, with a midwife, with pain medicine no more sophisticated than vocalizing and squeezing her partner's hand.

The idea of losing and gaining control is a pretty huge thing in our culture. We are told that with the right attitude and some hard work, we can master anything. If nothing else, it's a concept that sells a lot of books and keeps magazine writers busy. Skimming through some recent articles, book titles, and websites, I found instructions for controlling pretty much every aspect of our lives. There is an endless variety of "How to Control Your Weight" plans. Shrinks and self-help gurus offer pithy tips on how to control your anger, your anxiety, or your self-defeating thoughts. You can also learn how to control your diabetes, your flatulence, your credit card spending, your new puppy, your wife, or (my personal favorite, from *Popular Mechanics*) your runaway camel. (Apparently, you pull the reins to one side to make it run in a circle. Good to know.)

So we go through life in an eternal quest to grasp control of our careers, our relationships, our finances. We are constantly trying out new ways to control our bodies, through diet, exercise, yoga, Pilates, body-slimming underwear, and even cosmetic surgery. And then we come upon the totally new challenge of childbirth, and we have to decide: How important is it to me to exert control over this act? Is it possible, and do I really want to, after all?

In a way, we are all looking to impose some sort of control over childbirth. But do *you* want to call the shots, or are you happy to let your doctor take the reins? It really comes down to a philosophical choice between nature and science: *Do you want to control the emotional experience of giving birth, or do you want to control your body?*

For women who strive for an emotionally fulfilling birth

experience, control of their surroundings and the details of their labors is of utmost importance; they feel that creating comfortable, safe environments in which they call the shots will allow them to get out of the way of their bodies and let birth happen in its most natural and satisfying way. This could include the kind of music playing in the background, the specific rocking chair or tub they labor in, the positions they are allowed to assume when pushing, who and how many people can keep them company through the experience, what they can snack on and wear during labor, who gets to catch the baby when it comes out, and how soon they can hold and breastfeed the baby. They want to let nature, not technology, control the pace at which their labor moves along. But mostly, they want the power to veto any unnatural substances that are going to enter their bodies and reach their babies, or any artificial methods of coaxing their babies out. Their mantra seems to be, *My body, my baby, my choice, my control.* To other women, those details matter not a bit. *Sure*, they think, *it would be nice to labor in a cozy room drinking a smoothie, rather than in a bland hospital room sucking on ice chips,* but they will gladly trade all that in for the chance to exert some control over their physiology: inducing labor that is stuck in neutral, employing continuous fetal monitoring to make sure the baby is not in distress, considering surgical birth if the baby is having trouble making the journey the traditional way (or even if it's not), proximity to a neonatal intensive care unit (NICU) and, of course, the ability to medically control the pain.

This is where all those issues brewing in our lives come together: Without even consciously knowing it, we make choices dictated by our histories with doctors and pain, our trust or skepticism of science and technology, our basic philosophies of the body versus the mind, the influences of our families, friends, and the media, our feelings of independence or teamwork, our health insurance policies, our finances, our geographies, our faith in a higher power, our trust, our instincts, and our grit. And this is how we choose our place on the childbirth choices continuum.[14]

On the far left of the continuum, you have the women who choose to exert the most control over their experience and the least control over their physiology. On the far right are the ones who place the highest importance on medical intervention and the least importance on controlling the birthing atmosphere. As you slide across the continuum from one extreme to another, you'll come across all the different options, each one a shifting equation between the two different realms of control. And with each option, you give up one thing to gain something more important to you. The one thing that remains constant is that the women who make each choice believe that they are planning the safest possible birth for their baby. Here are the major stopping points along the way:

**Home birth:** Women who choose to deliver in the most old-fashioned, low-tech way possible have the luxury of writing all their own rules for their labor and birth, and they put a personalized stamp on the experience by dictating their surroundings. They believe that their baby is safest with the fewest possible medical interventions. But by choosing this path, they are also giving up the comfort of knowing that a potentially lifesaving operating room or NICU is just an elevator ride away.

**Independent childbirth center:** Cared for by midwives in a setting that strives to be as much like a home as possible, women who deliver naturally, without interventions, in birth centers, control their own experience—up to a point. While birth centers are far more mom-centric than hospitals, they still have their own specific protocols. The trade-off of giving birth in what is essentially someone else's home, and following their rules, is that you are closer, both physically and mentally, to the safety net of a hospital if something should go wrong.

**Natural birth in a hospital attended by a midwife:** Compromise for women who prefer the low-tech, hands-on, low-intervention, drug-free philosophy of a midwife but do not feel safe enough to deliver outside the hospital. In some hospitals, "natural labor" rooms are set up to facilitate this option.

**Natural birth in a hospital with an OB:** In a bid to have a natural experience without precluding the using of intervention and anesthetics, some women seek out doctors who will allow them to labor naturally (though most MDs will insist on some intervention if labor doesn't progress according to a predetermined timetable). These women often try to labor at home for as long as possible, thereby controlling the early part of the experience, and check into the hospital when they are closer to delivering.

**Vaginal birth in a hospital with anesthetics/interventions:** This is the most mainstream of all options, and it is the point on the continuum where *control over pain* takes on a starring role and the balance shifts, so that control of physiology starts to trump control of the birth setting (in fact, your attempt to create a cozy atmosphere may be watered down to whatever small details your hospital will allow, such as wearing your favorite pair of Kermit the Frog socks while you lie strapped to a monitor in a hospital-issued gown). Still, your body is given at least a fighting chance to deliver the baby vaginally, without surgical intervention.

> **NOTE:** All of the above options have the possibility of leading to a cesarean section after attempted labor, which, for the purposes of this discussion, does not count as a deliberate, predetermined choice. Though there are a few who moms say that they actually asked for a C-section after many futile hours of labor, others find themselves so physically and emotionally exhausted from pushing that when the doctor announces it is time to step up to a surgical birth, they can't do anything but silently nod as they are wheeled into the operating room.

**Medically advised, preplanned C-section:** Most women who schedule a C-section do so because their doctor is concerned about complications such as twins, breech position, or placenta previa, or because they had a previous C-section and are concerned about possible uterine rupture if they attempt a subsequent vaginal birth. A surgical delivery takes complete control of childbirth away from nature and hands it over to the physician. Control over atmosphere in an operating room is zilch. What do you gain in the process? Control over a situation that might have otherwise jeopardized your health or the health of your baby; control over the exact time and date of delivery; and control over pain during birth (though you trade that for a longer recovery period).

**Maternal-choice C-section:** At this point, we have reached the far right side of the continuum, the polar opposite of the intervention-free home birth. A growing number of women who have complication-free pregnancies are planning C-sections simply because they want to avoid the pain and possible physical complications of labor and control their own destinies. Since more than one in four births in the United States ends a C-section, whether or not the mother planned it that way, these women would rather make that decision, instead of having it thrust upon them after hours of laboring in vain.

What is so interesting to me is that the options in the middle of the spectrum, where you give up the most personal control by delivering in a hospital with the unpredictability of vaginal birth, are the most mainstream, acceptable choices in America today. The choices out on the far ends of the continuum, the ones where women truly examine their deepest needs and then exert the most control over either the experience or physiology of childbirth, are the most harshly criticized—by other women, by the press, and mostly by the mothers who've staked claim to one option over the other.

But as divided as the philosophies of natural birth and maternal-choice C-section are in the great debate over holistic versus medical birth, they do have one thing in common: The women who choose these options are making an unpopular, "radical" choice based on what they believe will empower them most. And no matter which childbirth option you pick, which spot on the continuum fits you best, isn't that the whole point—to come through childbirth stronger, proud of your accomplishment, and ready to tackle the even more challenging job of being a parent?

## CHAPTER THREE

# DOMESTIC DEBUTS: HOME BIRTH

*I* *had been having contractions all weekend. On Sunday night some friends came over to play cards, and then I went to lie down in the bedroom while they listened to music in the den. The baby must have really liked that music, because about an hour later, I felt a pop and my water broke. We called our midwife, who was really laid-back about the whole thing: She said she was going to feed the animals and then meander on over.*

*While we waited, my husband and I took a very slow walk down to the end of our road and back—the stars were out and it was really beautiful. Then we went back inside and lit some candles and put on my favorite Tom Waits album. My husband had painted the baby's name, Sophia, on the wall right next to a couple of paintings he had made, so I focused on that while he rubbed the small of my back. That helped a bit with the pain, which was bad, far worse than I had ever imagined. My mom and my midwife both arrived*

*around one-thirty in the morning, and at that point I got in
the tub, which felt so much better.*

*I let the water rock me and relax me while I listened to the
music, and I was able to control my breathing and focus on
pushing. I pushed for only a few minutes, and then my midwife said, "Reach down and touch your baby's head!" When I
felt her, I was so pumped. She came out in a rush. My husband
was in the tub with me, and he pulled her out and laid her on
my chest. It was the most amazing experience ever.*

**CHARLOTTE, FOURTH-GRADE TEACHER**
*LaGrange, Tennessee*

Oh, man, doesn't that sound sweet? The stars, the candles,
Tom Waits's gravelly voice guiding you through contractions
. . . the whole vibe of giving birth at home certainly has its
appeal, especially compared with the fluorescent lights and
institutional decor of most hospital delivery rooms. Yet this
laid-back, low-tech style of childbirth, a throwback to the
way it was done basically from the beginning of time to
about fifty years ago, inspired some of the angriest reactions
that I encountered in all of my research. When I asked some
moms who had given birth in hospitals what they thought of
home birth, some of the answers were downright hostile:

*"That is such a stupid idea. Moms who give birth
at home are just asking for trouble."*

*"Home birth is a great idea if you love pain! The only people I know who did that are the really earthy, crunchy, granola types."*

*"I think women who do this are selfish, illogical, and irresponsible. I realize that childbirth is a natural process, but it also comes with many risks for both mother and child. I actually find it disrespectful to all the women who have died in childbirth throughout history to completely turn away from the safety nets provided by modern medical science."*

And I have to admit, before I started tracking down home-birthing moms and midwives and lurking on their message boards, I had my own skeptical ideas about home birth, based on, well, pretty much nothing other than my own prejudices. None of my close friends had even considered the option, and in all the birth stories I had sat through at all the Gymboree classes and playgroups, the only one that took place in someone's home was the tale of a woman whose labor came on so quickly that she pushed out her child on her shower floor while her husband frantically dialed 911. It was clearly *not* how she had imagined that particular moment in her life. (It was only later that I realized there probably *were* a few home-birth moms in my extended network, but they weren't sharing their stories, for reasons I'll discuss later in this chapter.)

As for me, I could not fathom why anyone who didn't

live a six-hour horse-and-buggy ride from the nearest hospital would actually *choose* to go through labor and delivery in their own bedroom, without an MD present, without even the possibility of an epidural, without the constant reassuring presence of a fetal monitor, without every piece of modern baby-saving technology down the hallway *just in case.*

And that is what it all really comes down to. That is why we are all so hung up about the idea of anyone giving birth at home. It's not so much our skepticism toward why they would choose to suffer through the pain of natural birth, and it isn't even our disbelief that someone would want to mess up their own bedroom with the million different bodily fluids that accompany childbirth. It's all about the worst-case scenario: *What if something happens to the baby and you can't get to the hospital in time? How can a midwife be as prepared for emergencies as someone who spent all those years in medical school?*

Because the thing is, most of us spend our entire pregnancies in constant fear that something will go wrong. We scour the pregnancy magazines and health pages for the latest studies about how our diet and lifestyle will affect the baby. I have a visceral memory of the panic I felt one night when I was about five months pregnant with my second daughter. I had gone away by myself for the weekend to a convention in a nondescript hotel off the interstate in Connecticut. The first evening, I was enjoying a quiet dinner by myself in the downstairs restaurant when I realized, halfway through the meal, that I had misheard the waiter and the "codfish" I had thought I was eating was actually swordfish. I broke into a sweat and my brain raced, trying to remember what horrible birth defect eating this mercury-laden sea creature might bring. (So far, my three-year-old daughter seems to have suffered no ill effects from the swordfish, but if she gets cut from the soccer team in seventh grade, I suppose I can always blame it on the waiter with the incomprehensible accent.)

Throughout both of my pregnancies, I spent way too many hours debating the relative dangers of sushi, hair dye, and processed luncheon meat with other expecting moms. I pondered whether that glass of beer I drank before I knew I was pregnant would increase my risk of a miscarriage. I and all the pregnant women I knew felt this huge, overriding pressure that if we made one wrong move—god forbid we ate the wrong kind of cheese—we would mess this whole thing up. Like everyone else I knew, I dutifully read *What to Expect When You're Expecting,* which in its overarching, informative style, talked about every possible thing that could go terribly wrong. I lay awake at night, worrying that if I slept on my right side instead of my left, the baby wouldn't get enough oxygen. I worried about the baby not turning in time, about her getting stuck halfway down the birth canal; I read about Keanu Reeves's baby, who was stillborn just weeks before her due date. Starting in my sixth and seventh months of pregnancy, I would check BabyCenter.com every week or so to see what the odds were of my baby surviving if she were born that day. And believe me, I considered myself one of the more *relaxed* pregnant women I knew.

And then there are all the horror stories, dramatic narratives of emergency C-sections and babies in distress are the cautionary tales of modern motherhood. Everyone has one, about a cousin or friend or sister who was rushed into the operating room because the cord was wrapped around the baby's neck, the mother was bleeding, or the baby's heart suddenly, for no reason whatsoever, stopped beating. These stories all end with *The baby almost died,* or *The mother almost died!* Parenting magazines are filled with inspirational stories of babies who were born with drastic health concerns, only to be saved by the heroic staff in the delivery room. There's no question that these true stories are heartwrenching and make for great drama, but we tend to forget that they are extreme cases. The stories about normal, healthy deliveries rarely become the stuff of family legend or a three-page spread in a magazine.

So in the midst of this national obsession with *what if?,* the most radical thing in the world is to assume that everything will be just fine.

---

**Celebrity Home Births**

From cover girls to warrior princesses, these are a few celebrities who have given birth at home:

Cindy Crawford
Meryl Streep
Ricki Lake
Joely Fisher
Demi Moore
Pamela Anderson
Kelly Preston
Lucy Lawless

---

For me, the single most striking attribute of the women I talked to who chose to give birth at home was that they all shared a fundamental optimism about childbirth, a belief that it is a natural, healthy, *normal* process. Instead of letting their worries about pain or complications rule their experience (and they admitted to thinking about both), they focused on the positive and looked at the experience as a milestone to be excited about, rather than a nightmare to be endured. They made a conscious decision to reject what one mom called "the fear mentality," the idea that childbirth is an inherently dangerous undertaking that will end up in disaster unless a courageous doctor pulls you through.

And it's not that these women were naive about the possibility of complications—in fact, they were, as a group, incredibly eloquent and well-read on the topic. Each mom I talked to would tick off a long syllabus of the books she devoured in preparation for her home birth. The difference was, they were convinced that all the poking and prodding by doctors, all the anesthetics and inter-

*"My mother finally said, 'Well, okay, I guess you can do a home birth—as long as you have an ambulance parked outside!'"*

ventions, were responsible for *causing* many of those complications, rather than preventing them. They would quote studies, refer me to websites, and talk at length about the "snowball effects" of intervention. An epidural can slow down labor, in turn requiring Pitocin to speed it up. The Pitocin can slow the baby's heart rate, requiring internal fetal monitoring. And all these interventions can lead you down the path to a cesarean section.

They knew about all the "rules" in their local hospital, like how many hours a woman is allowed to labor after her water breaks, and whether continuous fetal monitoring and IVs are required. They were aware that most midwives have around a 10 to 15 percent rate of transferring patients to the hospital, and they were at peace with that. (I should mention that all the women I spoke to were otherwise part of the mainstream of American life. In certain religious groups like the Amish and some Mennonites, home birth is not so much a deliberate choice as a way of life.)

"We would rather assume that everything is going to go right, and focus on having faith in ourselves and in the process of birth," explained Caitlin, a yoga teacher and mother of one in Brooklyn, New York. "We definitely acknowledged that, yeah, if something goes wrong, I'm going to go to the hospital and I'm not going to fight it, but I will trust my midwife to know when it's time to go. Mostly we focused on how great it was going to be, and how we were doing it the way we wanted to." In fact, one midwife explained to me that as opposed as her clients were to the idea of a surgical delivery, they knew that if it came down to that, at least they would be secure in the knowledge that they had tried everything else and the C-section was absolutely necessary, rather than something that was forced upon them by impatient doctors.

As many of these moms pointed out, going through the most intense physical experience of your life in your own home is not for the weak of heart. So where did that extra edge of strength come from? A few of them did mention spirituality, but I found that their overwhelming faith wasn't in any particular religion, but in their own bodies. Janice, a stay-at-home mom of one in Chicago, told me, "I was going to write a birthing plan, but my midwife said to me, 'You don't need a plan, you have to just trust your body and let it happen.' And that took so much pressure away. Rather than trying to control everything, I just gave myself over to nature's plan."

And once you have this attitude that childbirth is a normal act of a healthy body, then it may seem unnecessary—counterintuitive, in fact—to have this act take place in a hospital, which for some people connotes illness and death. "A year after we were married, my husband's mother died, and we had spent a lot of time in a hospital," said Beth, a chef, writer, and mom of three in Brooklyn. "So I really got the feeling that hospitals were for sick people. It was just never clear to me why we have to give birth in them."

Of course, we can't have this discussion without addressing the question in the back of everyone's mind—*Is home birth really safe?*

Well, as with any emotionally loaded question about medical care, the answer depends on whom you ask. The American College of Nurse-Midwives will point out that multiple studies of thousands of women, including a 2005 report in the *British Medical Journal* that examined 5,000 planned home births,[1] have consistently found that if you are healthy and have had good prenatal care, with a full-term, low-risk pregnancy, giving birth in your own home is as safe as giving birth in a hospital and leads to fewer interventions. (The question about what is high or low risk is also open for debate. Most doctors and midwives would put anyone who is having twins, has had a previous C-section, or has a breech baby in the high-risk column, whereas I have spoken to midwives who argue that the only pregnancy that is truly risky is one where the baby or mom has previously diagnosed health problems, such as diabetes or preeclampsia, that need extra monitoring during labor.)

The American College of Obstetricians and Gynecologists and the American Academy of Pediatrics have a different take on the issue, however: "Because intrapartum complications can arise, sometimes quickly and without warning, ongoing risk assessment and surveillance of the mother and the fetus are essential," reads their coauthored *Guidelines of Perinatal Care.* "The hospital, including a birthing center within a hospital complex, provides the safest setting for labor, delivery, and the postpartum period. This setting ensures accepted standards of safety that cannot be matched in a home-birthing situation."[2] And some research, such as a 2002 study comparing planned home births and hospital births in Washington State published in the journal *Obstetrics & Gynecology,* indicates that there is a slightly higher rate of neonatal mortality (though it was still far less than 1 percent) for babies born at home.[3]

The debate about who is right could fill another book

entirely, but what is undeniable is that planned home births do have a far lower rate of intervention than hospital births and a rate of cesarean section that plummets to well below 10 percent.[4] For a woman with a certain mind-set and an uncomplicated pregnancy, home birth is a legitimate option, no matter how shocking it may be to everyone else.

So who are these brave souls, these childbirth optimists who suffer the slings and arrows of disapproval from friends, family, and complete strangers to give birth at home? Well, first of all, they are a very elite minority. In 2003, around 23,000 American babies were born in their mother's home, which amounts to roughly one half of 1 percent of all births in the United States[6] (in some European countries, like the Netherlands, interestingly, that rate is closer to 30 percent).[7] Though the midwives I interviewed report that their clients come from all economic and social backgrounds, research suggests home birth is primarily a choice of educated, middle-class women.[8] The women are also overwhelmingly white (0.6 percent of white babies were born at home, compared with 0.3 percent of black babies and 0.2 percent of Hispanic babies).[9] But it is a group that includes rural and urban women, younger and older moms, clerical workers and talk-show hosts (Ricki Lake was so inspired by her own home birth that she trained to be a doula).

## The thrifty choice?

According to one analysis, a home birth costs 68 percent less than a similar uncomplicated vaginal birth in a hospital.[5]

Each of these women, of course, has her own very personal reasons for delivering at home: Some didn't want to be apart from their older children; some wanted to give birth in the water; some wanted to attempt a vaginal birth after a C-section (VBAC) and couldn't find a hospital-based obstetrician to support them. There's the Mom factor, too: Some women did it because it's how their own mothers gave birth; others wanted to have an experience as *different* from her mother's as humanly possible. One woman I interviewed wanted to have the comforting presence of her two dogs, each weighing nearly two hundred pounds, in the room as she labored. A hospital, needless to say, would have frowned on this.

And while these women did not fit the vegan, hippie stereotypes I had imagined, there definitely was a nonconformist vibe to the group. Several of the moms I talked to were into yoga, mediation, and holistic medicine; one homeschooled her children. Heather, a welding instructor in Minneapolis, Minnesota, felt compelled to give birth at home to counter the sexism she encountered in her daily grind. "I work in a man's world," she explained, "and every day I come up against this totally skewed attitude of what being a woman is. I started to worry that it would take a toll on my self-esteem, and I needed to find out about what kind of strength I had in me. I also thought it was the healthiest option for both my daughter and me."

I was completely charmed by Charlotte, the soft-spoken teacher from Tennessee, who sheepishly admitted that she wasn't as brave as everyone thought when they heard she was giving birth at home. "I'm a big sissy. I don't like needles," she explained. "The idea of having a needle stuck in my back really scared me, and having my stomach cut open was just about my worst nightmare. I watched my mom give birth at home to my three younger siblings, and she was so calm and cool that I was never afraid of childbirth. Mom always talked about what a wonderful experience it was for her, and I figured whatever pain I had to go through was preferable to being in a hospital around all those needles."

Interestingly, many of these women told me they would have considered having their child at a birthing center—if there were one available to them. But, midwives tell me, since there are entire swaths of the country where there are no birth centers, few midwives doing hospital births, and a scarcity of MDs who support natural birth, many women come to the conclusion that their only chance of having a natural birth with no intervention is to stay at home.

But even women who have their choice of cozy, homey birth centers with Jacuzzis and floral-patterned rocking chairs still often decide to deliver their babies at home. "I toured a birth center at a hospital near me, but I found that when you come in, you have to go through triage. You have to be admitted and sit on the fetal monitor for twenty minutes before you can even go up to the birth center," said Caitlin. "The midwife who gave me the tour pulled me aside and whispered, 'If you really want to do natural birth, just do it at home.'"

While each home-birth mom's story was unique, I did start to sense a few themes: First of all, they are not so crazy about doctors. It's not that every home-birth mom I talked to actively *disliked* the medical profession (though a couple did express outright hostility); they just didn't buy into the whole idea of the MD as an all-knowing, larger-than-life, heroic figure. They certainly did not believe that a doctor knew more about what was going on in their body than they did.

"I was raised to be very skeptical about the medical establishment," says Laurie, a mom of two who runs a tutoring service in New York. "I think my father has been to a doctor only a few times in his life. My attitude is that I should use medical knowledge to my advantage with a thoughtful, educated approach, rather than being dictated by it. I respect what doctors know, but I don't think it's the be-all and end-all of what there is to know about the human body."

One mom told me she thought doctors were too quick to jump to pharmaceutical solutions before exploring natural remedies, and another one, after not being able to articulate why she distrusted doctors so much, suddenly flashed back to an incident when her mother brought her to an unfamiliar male pediatrician: "I went in complaining about a cough, and he ended up taking down my pants. I didn't understand why he had to look at my privates, so I pulled up my pants and ran out of the office with my mom right behind me. So the idea of going someplace filled with doctors was not my ideal situation." I couldn't help but compare that to my own experiences with doctors, and think of how that influenced my choice of where to give birth. I had a fabulous pediatrician who shared my passion for musical theater: Not only could she cure my strep throat, she could also regale me with tales of auditioning for the original off-Broadway cast of *You're a Good Man, Charlie Brown.* Then there was the college-clinic doc who introduced me to Advil. I didn't have a regular physician again until a few years later, when I searched for a simpatico gynecologist. After a couple of false starts with doctors I didn't quite click with, I switched to a doctor who was smart, compassionate, and occasionally took time off to work at women's health clinics in Africa. When I was pregnant, I actually looked forward to all those required checkups.

I now realize that all those warm experiences with friendly, caring female doctors helped steer me toward a medicated hospital birth. Had I not had the wherewithal to change practitioners when I wasn't satisfied with my care, or had I had a single unfortunate moment with a creepy doctor, then perhaps I would have felt compelled to interview a midwife or two. And if I had ever had a negative experience in a hospital, or spent any time with a grievously ill relative there, perhaps I would have thought to have my babies elsewhere. But the truth was, I was happy with the medical care I had received so far in my life and had no reason to consider giving birth in anything but the standard, expected way.

Another commonality that I noticed among home-birthers was that roughly half the women I talked to chose this option only after dutifully going to the hospital to deliver their first child and then walking away dazed, disappointed, and, in some cases, consumed with rage at the way it all went down. "I had my first child in the hospital, and we didn't want any intervention if at all possible," Heather told me. "But there was so much pressure to hurry up—at one point we were told that if I hadn't dilated to six centimeters by a certain time, they were going to burst my membrane. We were actually threatened, and that was not okay with either of us. Plus, there was construction going on in the building, and they were very insensitive about it. When I was laboring pretty heavy, I got in the bathtub, and it felt like the drilling was going on right underneath me. It made my pain-control methods completely ineffective."

Heather's experience of feeling pressured and "on the clock" at the hospital echoed the experiences of several of the women I spoke to. They felt the threat in the air: *If you don't hurry up and have that baby, we're going to cut you open.* I, too, remember the countdown at my daughter's birth: My water broke at 9:00 PM, and if the baby wasn't out within twenty-four hours, I knew there was a good chance the doctors would go in and get her (we made it with ninety minutes to spare). The theory is, once your water breaks, your risk of infection increases; home-birth moms feel that the risk of infection is only increased *outside* the home, in the foreign atmosphere of the hospital, with doctors introducing new germs every time they do an internal exam to see how far you're dilated.

Finally, what these mothers all had in common was that they wanted to experience birth in a deep, profound way. When you talk to women who had medicated births in a hospital (myself included), the general attitude is, *Let's get the labor over as quickly and painlessly as possible so I can get on to the good part: enjoying the baby.* For home-birth moms, the hard work of labor and delivery *is* the good part. They want to experience every last contraction, to feel the baby moving down the canal, to really understand how our bodies work, free of outside influences. They talk about moments of being scared and not knowing how they will get through it, but in the end, they all describe it as the most exhilarating and meaningful moment of their lives. They talk about the community—their partners, doulas, and midwives all working together to support their labor, rather than control it. One mom talked about squatting on her husband's lap in the final stages of pushing; another recalled how various female friends made appearances, massaging her legs and back and offering verbal support.

"At one point my husband was sitting on the edge of the bed, and I was squatting in front of him. Every time a contraction came, I pulled on his shirt, sort of like the rope-pulling Ina May Gaskin describes in her book to relax the lower half of your body. It totally worked! At one point I looked at my husband and said, 'Sorry I'm ruining your shirt,' but there was no way I was letting go."

And then there's the atmosphere. "There was nothing beeping in the background, no phones ringing. There were familiar smells; we had our favorite music; it really was peaceful," Penny, a graduate student in Madison, Wisconsin, explained. Instead of Mom being transferred to the maternity ward while Baby is transferred to the nursery, everyone chills out together on their family bed, with their favorite pillow, with the baby wrapped in a beautiful, handmade blanket instead of those glorified dish towels they have in the hospital.

"After I gave birth, the midwife went upstairs to make a cup of coffee and left us alone with the baby. My older son was in the kitchen with my sister, having breakfast. It was so nice," Beth told me. "When my third child was born, we realized very quickly that he had Down syndrome," she added. "Had he been born in a hospital, he would have been whipped away from me and tested, and I would have been left bereft and confused, like so many women I know who gave birth to children who are different. Instead, I celebrated when he was born."

While the atmosphere of home birth may be cozy, sweet, and peaceful, the attitude of the outside world peering in and making angry judgments about the moms is decidedly not any of these things. Everyone, it seems, has an opinion about home birth. "People literally roll their eyes when you tell them you are planning a home birth," said Heather. "They come right out and say, 'That is such a stupid idea.'"

Home-birth moms get attitude from all directions, but the first—and most hurtful—line of attack can often come from their family. Everyone who is connected to that child is going to feel some sort of protective instinct toward it. And if you happen to be giving birth to the first grandchild on both sides of the family, as I did, forget about it. That baby is seen as communal property. Unless you come from a family where home birth is a time-honored tradition, it is way off the map of what is considered normal twenty-first-century behavior. To get to the place where you feel empowered enough to try it, you have to go through a lot of soul-searching, but chances are, your family has not gone through that emotional process with you, so when you announce that you're planning a home birth, it can be like announcing you've joined some strange fertility goddess–worshipping cult.

The women I interviewed told me how the accusations, anger, and guilt trips came out in torrents, to a point where many of them just stopped talking to their family about the birth altogether. "My grandfather was totally opposed to a home birth, and he would hound me every time I talked to him," said Gina, a mom of one in Atlanta. "He thought it was dangerous. He kept saying, 'It's like going back to a horse and carriage when you already own a car!' Finally, I said I couldn't talk to him until after the baby was born, because it was just putting way too much stress on me."

For friends, acquaintances, and strangers in the street, safety issues surrounding home birth may be a valid concern, but the antagonism is rooted in something entirely different. There seems to be a palpable sense of contempt: *How can you be so sure everything will be fine? Do you think you are somehow so perfect and blessed that nothing bad will happen to you? How dare you be so calm about this?*

And, as many of the women reported, no matter how much research they did on the topic, everyone assumed they just woke up one day and said, "Hey, wouldn't it be fun to hang out at home, order in Chinese, and pop out a baby?" People accused them of making the choice out of ignorance, when, in fact, the opposite was usually true.

"I was working at the info desk at Barnes & Noble, and a woman asked me where I was having my baby," Caitlin recalls. "I told her I was doing it at home, and she said, 'Oh, I'm a nurse at St. Vincent's, and we had two home births come in last week.' I knew she wanted me to ask what happened, but I was like, 'Uh-huh, what book can I help you find?' I felt so angry. People are so judgmental."

After weeks or months of hearing people tell them how stupid, uncaring, and selfish they are, many of these women make a decision to just stop talking about it altogether. They avoid discussing it before the fact, because who wants to constantly defend something they are looking forward to, or even stand the possibility of being talked out of it? When people ask them where they are delivering, many of them get vague and say something like, "My midwife has privileges at a few places, and we're still deciding."

After the baby is born, when all the other mothers in town are going through their birth-story bonding ritual, they still tend to keep quiet about it (which may be why I never heard any home-birth stories, even though I live in a bohemian neighborhood where they are probably more common than usual).

All this silence can be incredibly painful, because so many of these women are so moved by their experience, they really do want everyone to know about it. "I was so thrilled with my birth, I just wanted to shout it from the rooftops," said Penny. "But I had to hold myself back because I just couldn't stand the look on everyone's face when I told them." Fortunately, with the ubiquity of message boards on every possible topic relating to childbirth, many of these women find like-minded moms to share their stories with online.

And there's yet another place where home-birth moms may have to confront negative attitudes from people who don't share their beliefs. That is the medical establishment that they have rejected, where, after all is said and done, they may wind up anyway. For the 10 to 15 percent of home-birth moms who get transferred to hospitals, the trauma of complications and the disappointment in not getting the birth they planned can sometimes be compounded by insensitive comments from doctors and nurses who more or less say, *Told you so.*

"My husband had to take a course with the midwives on what to do in an emergency," says Heather, "and that's when he asked them the most difficult question: What happens if it doesn't work out and we end up in the hospital and we're confronted not only with Heather and the baby possibly being in danger, but with all kinds of attitude from the hospital staff? Are they going to be respectful, or are they going to make us feel like we were stupid for trying a home birth?" Heather's midwife told them that was a legitimate concern, and other midwives have told me that they've seen doctors and nurses talking behind patients' backs and making condescending remarks about their attempt at a home birth. Yet, to be fair, I have also heard several stories of doctors who were nothing but considerate and kind to mothers who were transferred to their care.

While the women I spoke to each swore they would do it exactly the same way with any future children, they admit home birth is not always perfect and it's not for everyone. Both the midwives and moms agreed that certain criteria need to be met for someone to even entertain the idea of home birth.

You need to be prepared. Home birth is not something you should decide to do in your third trimester. You need to spend a good long time reading about it, understanding the implications, taking classes in pain-management techniques, and developing a trusting relationship with your midwife.

You need support. Home birth is generally not a great idea for someone who is going through the process alone. In all these stories, husbands and partners were major players, not only assisting the labor by massaging the mom, whispering words of encouragement, and cleaning pee and poop off the floor, but also by running interference with family members. Many of the women said that getting their husband to jump on the home-birth bandwagon took some time, but once he was there, he was as enthusiastic about it as anyone.

Finally, you need to feel safe. The whole point of home birth is to labor in the most comfortable, nurturing environment possible, so you can let nature do its thing. If you are going to tense up and worry about complications and have second thoughts about being outside a hospital, that safe haven is going to feel as comfortable as a concrete bunker.

Even if, like me, you don't think you could ever get to that mental and emotional place where you would feel completely safe giving birth at home, there is plenty to be learned in simply opening your mind to the idea. Andrea Christianson, a certified nurse-midwife in Tennessee, said it best: "Sometimes going to the extreme of considering a home birth allows a woman to think about what she wants in her birth, and what's important for her and her family, so that even if she chooses to deliver somewhere else, she can still ask for the most family-friendly, mother-friendly, baby-friendly birth possible."

## CHAPTER FOUR

# *The* BEST *of* BOTH WORLDS: BIRTH CENTERS

*I* *hate hospitals. I've really had some bad experiences in them before. Yet the idea of giving birth at home was way too scary for me. Luckily, when I was pregnant, I picked up a brochure from a birth center that was not too far from my apartment. It was beautiful, with rocking chairs and whirlpools and quilts hanging on the walls—it didn't have that sterile hospital look at all. It was more like a luxury suite at a hotel, and it was affiliated with a nearby hospital, just in case there were any complications.*

*I was on bed rest the last six weeks of my pregnancy, since I had been having early contractions, and I was getting stircrazy, but I knew I had to make it to thirty-seven weeks in order to qualify for the birth center. As soon as I hit that date, I was ready to samba. I decided to go out shopping just to get off the couch, and when I got home, I noticed that my pants were wet. We walked over to the center, where they tested the fluid; sure enough, I'd sprung a leak. They sent me home to try to get some sleep, and when we went back the next day, I did everything I could to bring on labor so I wouldn't go over the birth center's time limit. I tried cohosh, an herb that is supposed to induce labor, but it tasted terrible. Then I remembered hearing that a little romance could get things going, so I started kissing my husband, and all of a sudden it felt like my body dropped a water balloon on my feet.*

*As the waves started to build, my friend Paola, who had come for support, pushed on my lower back really hard, and that felt good. I was famished, so I ordered in a grilled-cheese sandwich and french fries, but I don't know what I was thinking—it all came right back up. Then the waves started getting really intense. At the peak of the contraction, I felt almost insane. I would try to breathe, but the only thing that helped was intoning AHHHH at the top of my lungs.*

*Pretty quickly, I started to feel the need to push. Somehow, I climbed into the birthing center's tub—it immediately felt right. I told my husband to sit on the edge of the tub; I got on my hands and knees like a frog and held on to him for dear life. The pain was pretty bad, and I remember saying, "I can't do this!" but the midwife and nurse said, "Yes you can!" and I gave one more push and the baby was out. I flipped around and scooped her up, and they put a blanket around her. We stayed there a while without cutting the cord—she was fine, I was fine, we were in this nice, warm tub, so there was no rush to cut it. After I got out of the tub, they weighed the baby and took a little blood. Then the three of us all got into the bed together. The baby was fussing and crying, and I couldn't sleep, though my husband had no problem—he was snoring away next to me. It was scary. I'd never had a baby before, and I didn't know what to do, but the midwife came in a couple of times and said, "It's okay, don't worry, she's just fine." Early the next morning, we strapped her car seat into a taxi and went home.*

**CATHERINE, ACTRESS AND MOTHER OF TWO**
*New York City*

The first year after my daughter Bellamy was born, I spent many, many hours at the Elizabeth Seton Childbearing Center on West 14th Street, which was one of the very first free-standing birth centers in the country. All the coolest moms in my neighborhood knew that Elizabeth Seton was the place to go for inexpensive Mommy-and-me music classes, postpartum yoga, and breastfeeding support groups. (Plenty of moms even schlepped their strollers on the subway all the way from Brooklyn to hang out there.)

For those of us who couldn't bear the thought of singing along with the hyperactive twenty-year-olds in polka-dot clown pants who led the local Gymboree classes, this was a welcome refuge, a place to be a mom without leaving your brain at the door. There were no fancy gift shops or state-of-the-art climbing structures there—we sat on the floor in the carpeted multipurpose room and paid for classes with crumpled ten-dollar bills. But the teachers were smart and laid-back, the classes were pleasant, and, a rarity in

Manhattan, moms actually outnumbered nannies. It was also something of a mini United Nations. Because midwife-assisted birth is so much more common outside the United States, it seemed that every expat mom residing in New York found her way to the center. Yes, we sang "The Wheels on the Bus," but in a melodious mix of Australian, British, Dutch, and Israeli accents.

In all those hours I spent shaking plastic maracas at Elizabeth Seton, however, I really never gave more than a passing thought to the fact that past the jumble of strollers, up the stairs, and behind closed doors, women were *actually giving birth*. Maybe their cries of pain were drowned out by all the moms singing Cat Stevens songs to their puzzled-looking two-month-olds, but still, it seemed way too calm a place for such a dramatic, life-altering event. In fact, the only hint that this wasn't just another branch of the YMCA was a corkboard I would glance at every time I parked my stroller. It was covered with Polaroids of disheveled, sweaty new moms, probably a couple of minutes after giving birth. They gazed at me through those photos, dazed and serene, holding tiny babies wrapped snugly in blankets.

I just assumed Elizabeth Seton would always be there, solid, no frills, dependable, in that red brick building next to the used-clothing store, as much of a neighborhood institution as the Spanish church down the block. But then two medical directors quit within months of each other, and soon the center's liability insurance was canceled. One day in 2003, a couple of months after my second daughter was born, the staff of Elizabeth Seton quietly packed up its birthing balls, took down those Polaroids, and closed their doors forever. And just like that, the 100,000-plus women who give birth in New York City every year[1] had one less place to do it.

I just took it for granted that there was a birth center within a fifteen-minute walk of my apartment, but it turns out that most American women are not so lucky. There are fewer than 200 independent centers across the country, and twenty-one states (including some pretty big ones, like New Jersey and Illinois) have none at all.[2] The numbers of women who give birth in them are tiny—fewer than ten thousand in 2003, which is about 0.2 percent of all women who gave birth in the United States,[3] and less than half the number of home births.

This microscopic number does not include women who delivered in "natural birthing" rooms within hospitals (see Chapter 6). What we're talking about here are freestanding, independent childbirth centers. They may have a financial relationship with a hospital, but they are autonomous, with their own set of protocols based on the guidelines of the American Association of Birth Centers (AABC).

The style of these centers varies widely across the country, depending on their local demographics: In some areas they have all the outward charm of a 99-cent store at a strip mall, and they serve a largely working-class, minority population. Others are so luxurious that a passerby might accidentally walk in and ask for a seaweed wrap and a facial. What they all have in common is that they aspire to be as unlike a hospital as possible, with kitchens and family rooms replacing operating rooms and NICUs. Some have MDs on staff as medical directors, but care is generally provided by midwives. What they don't offer is any kind of medical intervention (other than natural remedies like perineal massages and herbal treatments) or any of those painkilling drugs the rest of us beg for in the hospital. They are as decidedly low-tech as, well, giving birth in your own home.

The fascinating thing about birth centers is that they exist in a unique, very tiny little place on the childbirth-choices continuum. If you squint you can see them, hovering halfway between home birth and natural birth in a hospital. They offer an option that is neither as shocking to the general public as home birth nor as impersonal and medicalized as hospital birth. They hit all the right notes for a very select group of women, though clearly more would choose them if they were more accessible. In fact, the midwives I spoke with all had tales of women driving for hours, across state lines, just for the privilege of laboring in a birth center.

But the whole AABC philosophy of creating as domestic a setting as possible brings up an obvious question: If you want all the cozy and none of the chaos, and you're willing to brave it without any chance of getting that epidural, why not just stay at home after all? Why get in a car when you are in the middle of labor and travel to another place where their dearest wish is to make you feel as if you are right back in your own bedroom?

The moms I spoke to had all asked themselves that very

same question, and for many it just came down to this: The very concept of "home birth" was just a little *too* out there for them. For the most part, these were mainstream moms— there were corporate executives, PTA members, women who admitted that until their own pregnancies they had dismissed natural birth as something for "hippie moms who lived in Seattle." But after reading up about the high rate of C-sections, inductions, and episiotomies, or after having a bad experience with a medicalized first birth, they chose to go drug-and intervention-free, and they became convinced they wouldn't be able to achieve that goal within the high-tech confines of a hospital.

"I always assumed I would give birth at the hospital, since I didn't know anyone who had done it any other way," says Elly, a stay-at-home mom in Brookfield, Connecticut. "But a few years ago, I was diagnosed with fibromyalgia, and I was so sick I didn't think I would be able to go through a pregnancy at all. I finally turned to a naturopathic doctor, who diagnosed my symptoms as the result of the toxic buildup from all the allergy and migraine medications I had taken for years. Once I cleaned out my system, I got pregnant. But I knew that I didn't want to introduce any more drugs into my system if possible, so I started looking into alternative ways of giving birth. Through my doctor, I met other women who had delivered at birth centers, and it seemed like the perfect solution."

More than a few women used the same phrase: "the best of both worlds." They wanted some sort of free-form institution in which to give birth, but they didn't want their experience institutionalized. They wanted to be close enough to the hustle and bustle of a hospital—just in case—but they wanted the space they actually birthed in to be quiet and serene. Most of all, they wanted something that fit their personal parameters of what felt gentle, yet also completely safe. And even though the statistics suggest that for a low-risk pregnancy, home births and birth-center births have similar outcomes (the transfer rate at birth centers is between 10 and 15 percent, and roughly 5 percent result in C-sections[6]), there is something about walking out of your home and into a building with the word "birth" in its name that just *feels* safer. And, frankly, when it comes down to that animal instinct of hunkering down to give birth in a cozy environment, statistics and studies don't mean nearly as much as your gut feeling. It's not about logic, it's about how you feel—and the safer you feel, the easier your labor will be.

After all, we do a million different things at home every

---

## VBAC in a Birth Center?

Is it safe to attempt a vaginal delivery outside a hospital after a previous C-section? A 2004 study of more than 1,900 attempted VBACs in freestanding birth centers concluded that while the resulting complications were low and the success rate of vaginal births was high, the transfer rate of 26 percent and the increased number of risk factors made hospital care a safer option. Based on the results, the American College of Obstetricians and Gynecologists and the American Association of Birth Centers have recommended that women who attempt VBACs do so in a hospital.[4,5]

day—eat, work, argue, have sex, play Scrabble—but giving birth is not generally on the agenda. At a birth center, it *is* an everyday occurrence. Hundreds of women have safely brought their babies into the world there, and if *they've* done it, then it *must* be okay. It must be safe. There is a sense that birth is supposed to happen here. All those Polaroids of happy moms holding healthy infants spell it out for you. *Come here, join us,* they say. *If we did it, so can you.* Of course, along with all these intangibles of safety and comfort, there are many logistical reasons women choose birth centers over their homes. If you desire a water birth, that gleaming Jacuzzi may be a lot more appealing than your cramped bathtub or even one of the plastic birthing tubs you can rent. If you want to have every one of your seven siblings and their spouses attend the birth, they might fit better in the birthing center than in your studio apartment. A few women told me they didn't want to deal with cleaning up after the birth, and some said they just wanted to have their birth take place somewhere special and different.

## Water Babies

Delivering a baby in a bathtub sounds relaxing, but is it safe? One study of 1,600 water births concluded that women who chose this option had shorter labors and lower rates of episiotomy, and that there was no increased risk of infection.[7]

Women who deliver at birth centers understand that, just as with a home birth, there's a one in ten chance that their labor will stall or another complication will arise that will mess with all their plans and put them in the back of a taxi or ambulance heading to the hospital they hoped to avoid in the first place (though only a small fraction of those transfers involve life-threatening crises).

But here's the difference: The birth center has an ongoing relationship with a specific hospital, and the protocols for getting the patient from here to there are clearly established. If your home is a treacherous forty-minute ride from the nearest emergency room, but the birth center is two well-paved blocks from a major medical center, you have that much less to worry about as you lie awake at night pondering all the *what if?* scenarios. You don't have to think about the EMTs being delayed because they can't find your secluded house on a map or get through snow-covered roads that haven't been plowed. All systems are go. "I had seen a lot of ambulances get caught in traffic in my neighborhood," Catherine told me. "I could just imagine myself in the back of one, stuck behind a parade as the baby was coming out. At the center, at least I only had to make it around the corner."

If you ever want to get the warm fuzzies about where to give birth, go check out the websites for some of the country's birthing centers (you can link to every member of the American Association for Birth Centers at www.birthcenters.org). I swear, as I scrolled through the options, I felt like I was researching a romantic weekend for two in Vermont. You can take virtual tours of birthing rooms with four-poster beds covered with lace bedspreads, bathrooms with Laura Ashley curtains blowing in the breeze, handmade Moses baskets instead of plastic isolettes. There are snapshots of gazebos, patchwork quilts, potted plants, and bowls of pot-pourri. I assume there must be *some* evidence that childbirth happens there—perhaps a box of plastic gloves or some sutures—but all that is discreetly hidden away in distressed-wood hutches or carved armoires.

Still, while the women I spoke with did mention the lovely decor, I did not get the feeling that any of them signed up simply because of the Mary Cassatt prints hanging on the walls. All of these homey little details are simply the physical manifestations of a philosophy that strives for a warm, gentle atmosphere in which to greet your child for the first time. "I've been over to the hospital with friends who have delivered there, and it seems very cold and damp and not a very welcoming place to bring a newborn," said Michele, a mother of two in Shoemakersville, Pennsylvania. "At the birth center it was nice and calm and quiet. It was really such a warm atmosphere."

And that whole calm, loving attitude starts with prenatal checkups (birthing centers offer health care for the entire nine months, plus well-woman care afterward). A big selling point for these moms was the idea of collaborative care. They wanted to feel they were in partnership with their midwives, rather than just being an anonymous patient rotating through the system, being poked and prodded for tests they didn't ask for or even understand.

"One of the things I really appreciated about the center was that there was a level of respect for the mom you just don't find in a doctor's office," said Asha, a teacher in Bethesda, Maryland. "You take on the responsibility for your own care."

Some women also appreciated that prenatal screenings such as amniocentesis and blood tests were discussed and offered as options, but that they didn't feel pressure to have any tests that they didn't want. They liked the fact that they were being treated as a healthy woman having a checkup, not as a patient with an illness that had to be treated.

Just like the home-birth advocates who feel that women are manipulated and manhandled by a medical system that puts the needs of the doctor ahead of the needs of the patient, women who choose birth centers expressed a strong desire to be in control of their care—to call the shots as much as possible, without having to follow what they feel is an arbitrary set of rules.

It's not like a birth center is just one big free-for-all, however. There are actually quite a few strictly enforced rules. Unlike home births, which are not regulated by anything other than the judgment of the midwife overseeing your care, birthing centers have fairly strict rules about who can deliver there. Only the lowest-risk pregnancies are welcome, which means you will be screened for health problems like seizure disorders or diabetes and other risk factors, like twins or previous C-sections, at your very first appointment; if there's anything that puts you in the AABC's risk category, the midwife will refer you to a hospital for your delivery—though she may agree to continue as your health care provider and can deliver your baby if she feels qualified to do so in your case and has hospital privileges. Your level of risk is reassessed at each prenatal appointment, and if your baby is stuck in breech position, you develop preeclampsia, or your labor begins before thirty-six weeks or after forty-two weeks, you get sent right over to that hospital delivery room.

*"I was thirteen days late and knew I wouldn't be allowed to deliver at the birth center if I went past forty-two weeks, so I induced myself by drinking castor oil! It made me completely sick, but it eventually worked. I had a five-hour, unbelievably intense birth, but it was natural and beautiful and wonderful."*

But let's say you have a single-baby, full-term pregnancy and you get through each of your prenatal exams without "risking out" of the birth center. Good for you— now you are in charge of the details of your delivery. If you want to run around the room buck-naked, singing Puccini arias while the pom-pom squad from the local high school cheers you through each contraction, go right ahead. Unlike in a hospital, where you are often confined to your bed and attached to an IV and a fetal monitor, at a birthing center you are free to move around as much as you want. In a hospital, the baby is usually taken to the nursery and returned to the mom when the doctors deem her "ready"; at the birthing center, mother and child are never separated.

And let's talk about one of my favorite topics—food. When I was going through my long, long labor with my first daughter, I was not allowed to eat anything, not even a little nibble of the granola bar I had optimistically thrown in my bag as we left the house. So when the baby finally came out and I was moved to the maternity ward at 11:00 PM, I was absolutely famished, as if that six-pound space in my belly that the baby had just vacated needed to be refilled immediately, with bread and cookies if possible. "Sorry," the nurse said, "the cafeteria closed a couple of hours ago." Luckily, I live in New York City, land of the twenty-four-hour bodega, so I sent Jeremy out, wandering the streets in search of a tuna sandwich and a Diet Peach Snapple. I scarfed down a couple of bites before the exhaustion finally hit me. When my food tray arrived the next morning with a sad little box of dry cereal and some questionable-looking fruit, I realized that all those hoary jokes about hospital food were frighteningly accurate.

At birth centers, however, you are free to eat whatever you want, whenever you want. There are stacks of takeout menus, just in case you crave some postpartum kung pao chicken. The kitchen there is at your disposal—or more likely, at your family's disposal. "I could have eaten during the labor if I wanted to, but it went too quickly," said Elly. "Once it was done, I was like, 'Give me some food *now!*' My mother-in-law brought trays of her delicious homemade pasta and heated it up in the dining room upstairs from the birth rooms. She brought the plates in for me and my husband, and we ate it right there in the room with the baby sleeping next to us."

Hmm, soggy tuna in a cramped hospital room versus Mom's lasagna in a private hotel-like suite? Score one for the birth center.

So I love all that—the idea that you can eat whatever you want; that you don't have to share a room with a stranger (why did my roommates always feel the need to call their hearing-impaired grandparents just as I was nodding off?); that your husband can curl up in the double bed with you, rather than trying to sleep in a metal folding chair. But as idyllic as a birth center sounds, still, there are some details that give me pause. The first is the travel thing. With my second delivery, getting myself from my apartment to the hospital was an exercise in pure torture. When I woke up with what I thought were gas pains at 3:30 AM, I was already heavily into labor. It seemed that every time I tried to take a step out to the street to hail a cab, a contraction would hit, stopping me dead in my tracks. Speeding up First Avenue in the back of a taxi, hitting every pothole while an imaginary python tightened around my waist, was truly the innermost circle of pregnancy hell.

When we arrived at the hospital ten minutes later, the contractions were so intense and so close together that I could barely get out of the taxi. The only thing that kept me from sitting right down there on the curb and letting the cab driver deliver the baby was the promise of the epidural awaiting me through those revolving doors. So if I had decided from the start that I was going to have an unmedicated, midwife-assisted birth, I'm convinced that I would have said, *To hell with it. I'm not moving anywhere. You come here to my house.*

And it's not like you can just mosey on over to the birth center the moment you feel the slightest twinge of labor and then hang around, waiting for the hard part to hit. All birth centers have time limits on how long you can labor there—after either twelve or twenty-four hours, you "time out" of the center and get transferred to the hospital (mainly because stalled labor is more likely to require intervention, which the center does not provide). So if you go early, before you are in the thick of labor, they are probably just going to send you back home.

"I went to the center a few hours after my labor started, but they sent me home," says Elly. "After another three or four hours, I was sure things were happening. But when we went back, I was still only at two centimeters. The midwife told me, 'You can stay if you want, but we'll have to send you across the street if it takes more than twelve hours.' So I got back in the car and drove to my Mom's house, which was closer to the center. As soon as we pulled into her driveway, my water broke. We should have just turned right back around, but I wanted to make sure I didn't go over the time limit. Pretty soon, though, I started to feel the urge to push, so we went back, and when they checked me, they said, 'Honey, if you want that water birth, you'd better get in the tub right now, because the baby is coming!' "

And that clock doesn't stop ticking once you have the baby: Post-delivery, you have only a few hours before you are politely asked to pack up and leave. Women who have done hospital births, who are used to staying in the maternity ward for at least two days, are generally stunned by this fact. It's not that I loved—or even liked—being in the hospital, but there is something to be said for having a team of nurses overseeing your baby's health for a couple of days while you get used to the idea of being in charge of a whole new human being. At a birth center, it generally goes like this: If you have the baby during the day, you leave before night falls. If you have the baby in the middle of the night, you pack up the next morning.

Now, while other moms I mentioned this to were fairly shocked by the quick-exit policy, midwives and birth-center moms swore up and down that the type of woman who would choose a birth center would have it no other way. "I've had women who deliver at noon, and by 2:00 PM, they're looking at the clock, saying, 'Can I go home now? My older kid will be getting off the bus soon,' " one midwife told me. "We visit them at home the next day, so it's not like we're saying, 'Goodbye and good luck.' "

True, almost all the women I spoke with said they were eager to get back home, into their own comfy bed. Since they were not recovering from surgical births and they weren't feeling the effects of any anesthetics, they all said they felt fine walking out mere hours after giving birth (though if they were anything like me, it was more of a waddle than a walk for the first couple of days). "Yes, I was a little sore," Asha explained, "but I had so much adrenaline left over from the excitement of the birth that I couldn't sleep, and I just wanted to go home and start my new life with my baby."

There's the excitement of going home—and then there's the reality of *being* home. As Lila, a development manager for IBM in Dallas, said, "You go home and you have this six-hour-old baby, and you are completely responsible for its care. You need to be mentally ready for that. It's a whole other level of anxiety." Which is why every last mother and midwife stressed how important it was to have a support system at home if you choose to go the birth-center route. Partners who were taking time off from work were crucial, as were the SWAT teams of mothers, sisters, and in-laws ready to swoop in and give the baby a bath while the new mom took a nap.

"We were home within three hours after each of my babies was born," says Gayle, a chiropractor in west Los Angeles. "But my husband was around, and my mom was there, and she was totally helpful. I knew I could lean on both of them. As a new mom, you need to recover and take care of your baby, so if you don't have close family or friends who will be there for you, then you're probably better off delivering in a hospital, where you will have nurses to help you out."

Moms who successfully give birth at independent birth centers tend to be delighted—almost evangelical—about their experience. But what does the rest of the world think of this unique option?

First of all, because birth centers are so few and far between, most people don't know enough about them to have an informed opinion. They picture them as a throwback to the 1960s, a commune of squatting moms in love beads doing primal screams while midwife-shamans chant and burn incense. At the very least, most people know it's not a hospital, and that can't be good. One twenty-four-year-old woman I spoke to put it rather bluntly: "I think the whole idea of birthing centers is stupid. All that emotional, hand-holding stuff, the candles and the doulas, it doesn't mean a thing if something goes wrong."

Interestingly, while the skepticism is definitely there, it is less in-your-face than what the home-birth moms experienced. Only a few of the birth-center moms I spoke to complained about getting verbally attacked by people who didn't agree with them. ("The reactions were more like, 'Wow, that's interesting—but there's no way *I'd* ever do it,'" Gayle told me.) There is a grudging respect for the fact that this is some kind of organized movement, rather than just one lone mom going off on her own to have a child.

But poke through that outward politeness of "Fine, whatever works for you," and you'll find some of the same roiling resentment—*How dare you take that chance with your child?*—that other moms feel about home birth.

When I asked several hospital-birth women for their honest, uncensored opinion about birth centers, I got some interesting responses. Many moms—especially those who tried for natural birth in a hospital—admired the ones who avoided the hospital altogether, and they even sounded a little envious. But they still had major doubts about how safe it really was. Others, particularly those who had had complications with their own births, were way more negative: "It's reckless and dangerous," a mom who gave birth to two children in a hospital said to me. "In so many instances, medical intervention needs to be done immediately to have the greatest chance for success, and that can't exactly happen if you're busy schlepping a woman in labor from the birth center to the hospital. You can call it whatever you want, but it is still the same thing as home birth."

This muted, slightly more respectful brand of disapproval turns out to be a significant reason why many women who could have birthed at home went for the more socially acceptable option of a birth center. It certainly is true that for many women, home birth was never a serious consideration. They saw it as an overly radical choice or simply, as one or two moms said, "for women who are a lot braver than I am." If they hadn't been fortunate enough to find a center nearby, they probably would have toughed it out in the hospital. But for others, the choice seems to be less a resistance to the idea of home birth itself, and more a reluctance to deal with the onslaught of negativity that would rear its head as soon as "home birth" entered the conversation.

"Home birth was actually my first choice," admitted Lila, "but my husband was concerned about what people would think. He said, 'If anything went wrong with you or the baby, people would look at me and say, "Why did you let her stay at home?"' I knew how much pressure he would feel, and I knew I couldn't do it unless he was completely on board. So the birth center seemed like the next-best choice." Other mothers mentioned how helpful it was to take their families on tours of the center, or how they were able to toss out certain factoids—like the presence of an obstetrician who reviewed all the charts, or the center's location across the street from the hospital—every time concerned friends questioned the wisdom of birthing there.

But let's not paint a deceptively rosy picture—even though skeptical families may be partially appeased, they still hold their collective breath, not quite believing that everything will be fine until they see a squealing baby emerge from the room.

"When I started talking about the birth center, I knew my mom was freaking out," said Diane, an administrative assistant and mother of one in San Francisco. "She couldn't believe I wasn't going to use a doctor. But I think she knew if she acted all worried, it would make me dig my heels in even more, so she tried to act completely neutral. Underneath, I knew she was nervous as hell."

Because birth-center moms straddle two opposing sides of the childbirth debate—"safer at home" and "safer in the hospital"—they really seem open to the idea that there is a spectrum of legitimate choices, and that each woman has to find her own comfortable place in it. I found that as a group, they were the least judgmental about how other mothers chose to deliver their babies. "You need to do whatever it takes so you come out happy and the baby comes out healthy," says Gayle. "I don't think there's a right or a wrong, and I don't place a value on it. The birth center was the right choice for me, and we're fortunate that everything turned out fine, but if you can't do it because you're high-risk, or if philosophically you want to do drugs and avoid the pain, then I've got no problem with that."

And instead of being wary about sharing their story with other mothers who might disapprove, birth-center moms seemed eager to tell their tales to the whole world. It was as if they have discovered a wonderful, hidden secrets—an idyllic setting for a momentous occasion. They know it's not for everyone, but they want everyone to have the chance to at least consider it. "The whole process has been such an education for me, and now I want to educate other people about it," says Lila. "I try to drop it into the conversation wherever I can: I'll be talking to another mother and say, 'Blah, blah, blah, my midwife told me . . .' And I'm just waiting for them to say, 'Really? You delivered in a birthing center with a midwife? Tell me all about it.' "

## CHAPTER FIVE

# FROM BABY CATCHERS TO BIRTH COACHES: MIDWIVES *and* DOULAS

I will now take a moment to confess that the first time I heard about birth centers—roughly eight years ago, when a pregnant woman who lived in my building told me she was planning to deliver in one—the first shock wave that jolted my brain wasn't about the no-drugs policy or the possibility of giving birth underwater, it was all about my neighbor's nonchalant confirmation that a midwife, rather than a doctor, would be assisting in her delivery. *A midwife?* I thought. *Are they still around? Are they safe? Are they legal? Does your doctor know about this?* Jeez, my grandmother, a working-class immigrant from Eastern Europe, gave birth to my father in the back room of their Brooklyn tenement in 1933—but even *she* scraped together enough money to hire someone with a medical degree to come by and catch the baby.

Before I began writing this book, I had some vague idea that midwives existed, but I had very little idea about who they were and what they did. The very word itself seemed arcane, an unfortunate aural amalgamation of "medieval" and "housewife" (after a little research, I discovered it's actually Old English for "with woman"). The only time the word "midwife" ever flashed into my conscience during my two pregnancies was when I flipped through the first chapters of *What to Expect When You're Expecting* and skimmed a brief section on different types of practitioners, which included certified nurse-midwives and direct-entry midwives, along with obstetricians and family-practice physicians. *I guess they're covering all their bases,* I thought. But really, in this day and age, how many women actually use a midwife?

Actually, quite a few.

After midwives were pretty much pushed off the childbirth landscape by insurance companies, hospitals, doctors—and women's preferences—in the middle of the twentieth century, they've have had a resurgence in popularity over the past thirty years, and the 7,000 or so certified nurse-midwives practicing in the United States now attend around 8 percent of all American births.[1,2] (Between 1975 and 1995 alone, there was an increase of more than 1,000 percent in births assisted by a certified nurse-midwife, from just under 20,000 to 229,000.)[3] And after speaking to dozens of women who not only went out of their ways to choose midwives, but who were rapturously happy with the quality of their care, I have completely changed the way I think about one of the world's oldest professions. (Of course, just as not everyone loved their doctor, I found plenty of women who were not thrilled with their midwife—but more on that in Chapter 11.)

Yes, I had expected to hear that midwives were caring, nurturing, and supportive throughout pregnancy and labor, but I was surprised to hear all the stories about how calmly and efficiently midwives dealt with minor crises that the mothers felt would have automatically created an "emergency" atmosphere leading to unnecessary interventions had they been treated by a doctor.

"As soon as my baby's head came out, we saw that the cord was around his neck," recalled Elly, who delivered her son in a Connecticut childbirth center. "I wasn't too concerned, because my midwife had already explained that this happens a lot. She was very calm and just said, 'Okay, we've got a cord around the neck, hang on for a minute.' Before I knew it, I could literally feel her stick her pinky in there and pull the cord over his head, and then a minute or two later, I pushed him right out. I had been in the hospital with my sister-in-law when she gave birth, and the cord was also wrapped around her baby's neck, but the difference in the way they handled it was like night and day. The doctor said, 'Don't push!' and then he clamped the cord and cut it, and the poor kid came out blue! I *knew* he would be blue, because—*duh!*—they cut off his oxygen!"

Of course, every birth is different, and it's impossible to

tell what would have happened in either of those cases had the midwife or doctor reacted differently, but Elly explains that it was the serene, panic-free atmosphere that made all the difference to her: "With the doctor, it was like this big medical emergency, but my midwife saw the cord around the neck as just a natural variation on birth. She said, 'Well, if you give a kid a jump rope that long and let him play with it for a few months, of course it'll wind up around his neck!'"

(Quick test: When you read the previous quote, were you concerned at the midwife's casual reaction to the cord around the neck, or were you impressed with her commonsensical approach? Keep that gut reaction in mind as you choose the most appropriate practitioner for yourself.)

Despite the growing numbers of certified nurse-midwives in this country, and despite their bulging Rolodexes of satisfied customers, midwives still struggle with an outdated public image. I was far from the only woman who assumed that midwives were a vestige of Ye Olde Birthing Days, when having a baby meant biting down on a rag while squatting on a dirt floor. In a completely unscientific experiment, I asked twenty women who had delivered in a hospital with a doctor to tell me the first thing that popped into their head when they heard the word "midwife." Here are some of their answers:

> *"I think of the midwives Shifra and Puah from the Bible—I always loathed those names. I also think of pain, standing on bricks, and possibly dying in childbirth."*

*"I think of 'medieval,' which reminds me of knights and armor and way-old-fashioned birthing."*

*"The first word that comes into my mind is 'headscarf'! I know that sounds ridiculous, but 'midwife' makes me think of a farmer's wife laboring by candlelight in a log cabin out on the prairie."*

*"I guess the picture that pops into my head is one of a woman in extreme pain, pushing a baby out in a tiny room onto bloody sheets. I would never use one. I am totally for up-to-date medical practices and want a trained doctor in a big hospital with tons of backup."*

*"Midwife—would that be the second or third of Johnny Carson's four wives?"* [Yes, every focus group has to have at least one class clown.]

Even the more charitable responses I got—the ones that weren't filled with images of blood and pain—still included the disclaimer that as lovely as the idea of a midwife sounded in the abstract, they weren't something these women had considered as a legitimate option.

*"Midwives hold your hand, chant relaxing things in your ear, swab your sweaty forehead, and encourage you to go the distance without drugs. I wouldn't*

*think of using one because I believe that between the nurses at the hospital, my husband, and my OB, I should have all the encouragement I need!"* [This woman clearly had midwives confused with doulas, a common mistake that I'll discuss later.]

When I read some of these comments to the midwives I interviewed, they were not surprised. In fact, when I asked Deanne Williams, the executive director of the American College of Nurse-Midwives (ACNM), if there had ever been any discussion of updating the name "midwife" to something more contemporary-sounding, she sighed and said, "That conversation has been going on since the 1920s, when we first professionalized and set national standards. But the horse is out of the barn. Besides, what are the alternatives? If you change it to something like 'physician's assistant' or 'obstetric assistant,' the core philosophy about what midwifery is all about is going to be lost."

So there it is. Midwife. Not "natural-birth facilitator," not "associate director of human delivery," not even "reproductive systems administrator." Midwives know who they are, they know their history, and they proudly stand by their title and the ideals behind it.

For the rest of us, however, the facts are a little murkier. I found that unless a woman was acquainted with a midwife when she was growing up, had a predisposition to holistic healthcare in general, or had done a lot of reading on the topic when she found out she was pregnant, her knowledge of midwifery care was probably as narrow as mine had been. The women I spoke with who had delivered their babies with physicians had questions about what kind of training midwives had and whether they were allowed to practice in hospitals. Many people assumed they had no real medical background and were simply there to provide labor support, much like a doula.

Here are the facts: Certified Nurse-Midwives (CNMs) are legal and licensed to deliver babies in all fifty states. To earn your CNM license, you must have a nursing background and at least a bachelor's degree (over 70 percent hold a master's or a doctorate). You also must graduate from a nationally accredited midwife-training program and pass the ACNM's qualifying exam. A newer title, Certified Midwife (CM), was created in 1997 by the ACNM to give national certification to midwives who do *not* have a nursing background. A CM must still have a bachelor's degree, including core science classes, and must pass the same exam as CNMs. There are only a handful of women with this new title so far, and they have yet to gain legal recognition in every state. Both CNMs and CMs practice primarily out of hospitals.[4,5]

Then there are so-called direct-entry midwives, who learn their trade through apprenticeship, rather than a formal degree program. These midwives are on much shakier legal ground—as of this writing, they were illegal in eleven states, including Missouri and Illinois, and in an unlicensed gray area in many others.[6] In 1994, a movement to professionalize these women led to yet another new title: Certified

Professional Midwife (CPM). A woman who has paid her dues assisting another midwife can earn her CPM stripes by either demonstrating her skills in a practical exam or completing an accredited midwifery program.[7] Direct-entry midwives, who practice mostly in rural areas and assist mainly in home births and birth centers, come closest to that stereotype of the lone practitioner out on the prairie, but their track record is actually quite impressive: A study published in the *British Medical Journal* in 2005 found that North American women who had home births with CPMs in 2000 had no greater risk for maternal or infant mortality than women with low-risk hospital births, and their rates for interventions were extremely low (12 percent were transferred to hospitals; 3.7 percent resulted in C-sections; 2.1 percent had episiotomies).[8]

I was quite surprised to learn that 97 percent of the deliveries attended by CNMs are inside a hospital.[9] I was not surprised to find out that this is a profession made up almost entirely of women, though there are approximately seventy male midwives shattering stereotypes in delivery rooms around the country.[10]

So midwives are everywhere. They're attending home births for Mennonite women in isolated farmhouses; they are massaging the backs of laboring businesswomen in swanky birthing centers; and they are attending to Medicaid patients in urban hospitals. But what all these diverse women (and the few men) have in common is this: a belief in the absolute normalcy of childbirth.

Whereas doctors are trained to anticipate every possible thing that could go wrong with childbirth—which is ultimately what is so comforting for those of us who can't help but imagine the worst—midwives are trained to assist in low-risk natural births. Which is not to say they are not prepared for the occasional emergency, says Williams. "If you know normal like the back of your hand, then you recognize very quickly what's abnormal," she explains. "If we see that something is going wrong, then we consult with or refer the patient to an obstetrician who cares for the abnormal. Many times the problem only requires a minor intervention, and you can still continue under the midwife's care. But we do recognize that for women with known risks, such as multiple pregnancies, problems with their blood sugar, or placentas growing in the wrong place, they absolutely need to see a high-risk obstetrician."

*"With my second child, I was dilated four centimeters on my due date but hadn't started labor yet. My midwife asked if I was ready to have the baby, and when I said yes, she used acupressure massage to naturally induce labor. She basically squeezed my calves, knees, and thighs at three different pressure points, and said, 'You'll be in labor in four or five hours.' I was like, Okay, whatever, hippie midwife. But that's exactly what happened!"*

Of course, the philosophy of childbirth's being a normal, healthy function is inevitably tied to the belief that childbirth succeeds best at its own pace, meaning that there are as few interventions as possible and no artificial painkillers. "I liked that my midwife wasn't all about medicine and intervention," says Michele, a Pennsylvania mom. "During my labor she was there saying, 'Okay, your back is hurting, let's try something different. Why don't you get you up on your knees?' I felt like she could relate to my pain and help me feel confident that I could do this."

But as much as you're grooving on the idea of natural childbirth, if you give birth in a place where drugs are an option (meaning not in your own home or an independent birthing center), in your twentieth hour of labor, that epidural might start looking very attractive. Chances are, your midwife will try to talk you out of it, but if you truly want one, she shouldn't stand in your way. "We know there are many good reasons a woman might want pain relief," Williams acknowledges. "And we will make sure the epidural is used judiciously, so it doesn't create a cascade of events that ends in a C-section. Even though we are experts in caring for women who want unmedicated childbirth, women who want epidurals can still benefit from midwifery care. It is not just about childbirth—you are pregnant for many more hours than you are in labor, and how women are treated and what they know during pregnancy has a lot to do with their physical and emotional well-being."

I've found that people who are skeptical about midwives are entirely focused on the big-ticket event—the actual delivery of the child. But the women who choose midwives rhapsodize just as much about the care they receive before and after the big day. In their pre-conception, prenatal, and postpartum visits, they thrived on the personalized attention that they say is impossible to find in the rush-rush, assembly-line atmospheres of many hospitals and medical practices. They also liked the balance of power—rather than being made to feel like a helpless child who shouldn't question Big Daddy Doctor's practices, they felt they were partners in collaborative efforts with their midwives.

"My midwives let me set the pace at my checkups," says Gina, who had an OB deliver her first child in a hospital and a midwife deliver her second at a birth center. "I would weigh myself and then write down the number for them, and I would pee on the stick and check that myself. They asked me each time if I wanted an internal exam, whereas with a doctor they just go right in without asking."

All of the moms I spoke with who had switched to midwives after a more mainstream experience mentioned how shocked they were at the amount of time the midwife spent with them—quite a difference from sitting in a brightly lit, uncomfortable waiting room for an hour or more to see a doctor for five minutes. They also loved the holistic approach to care, where they were asked not just about their blood tests and weight gain, but about their hopes and anxieties, their mother-in-law issues, and their favorite banana-bread recipe.

"Since I did a home birth with my second child, my midwife came to me for prenatal visits," said Laurie, a Brooklyn mom whose first child was delivered in a birth center. "It really feels like your buddy is coming over and helping you out. She meets your kids, hangs out in your kitchen, you have tea. It's two people having a relationship! It's such a different paradigm. Now it's totally uncomfortable for me to go to a doctor's office for my annual Pap smear. It feels like I'm going through this weird ritual, and the doctor seems so bored. I respect why doctors do it that way, but I think I really got spoiled by having a midwife."

Of all my preconceived notions about midwives, one was actually right on the money: They *have* been around forever. Back in the cavewoman days, the few career choices available included hunter, gatherer, and midwife. Not that they were actually hanging up shingles and dealing with HMOs, but the role of an older, experienced woman helping another woman through childbirth is universal and timeless.

After I heard the response about midwifery evoking biblical images of Shifra and Puah, I went to my bookshelf and pulled out a paperback copy of the Old Testament to search for their story. There they were, in Exodus 1:15, two feisty heroines who outsmarted the pharaoh. When he ordered the "chief Hebrew midwives" to kill all Jewish boys immediately after birth, Shifra and Puah made up a quick lie: "Sorry, boss. The Jewish women are too fast for us; they pop out those babies before the midwife even gets there. Nothing we can do." Midwives have been looked at alternately as angels and pariahs ever since.

There are scholars and writers who paint glowing pictures of early midwives as kindly earth mothers who believed in letting nature take its course and did little more than wipe the laboring woman's brow, change the mound of straw or grass that she squatted on, and gently bring the newborn baby to her breast.[11] Other academics, however, claim that midwives weren't always quite so hands-off, frequently using their fingers to stretch the woman's labia or apply ointments to the perineal tissue or tugging at the baby's head and the placenta. There is historical evidence that some midwives would carry a dirty birthing stool from house to house, spreading deadly germs, or use an unwashed fingernail or pointed thimble to rupture the woman's sac. Clearly, as in any line of work, there were seasoned professionals and rank amateurs, and records suggest that in urban areas, midwives were organized and self-regulating and had standardized procedures for dealing with complications; whereas in rural areas, midwives tended to have little training, usually worked alone, and may have been less prepared to deal with emergencies.[12,13]

The concept of a medically trained and licensed nurse-midwife didn't take shape in the United States until early in the twentieth century (we had nurses and we had midwives, but little cross-pollination). In the 1920s, when directors of New York's Maternity Center Association (MCA), which provided prenatal care to mothers in poor neighborhoods, questioned why England and France had far lower rates of maternal and infant death than the United States, they zeroed in on those countries' reliance on nurse-midwives. So a group of public-health nurses from New York were shipped over to England for training, and in 1931 the MCA opened the first schools for nurse-midwifery in the United States. Meanwhile, over in the mountains of eastern Kentucky, Mary Breckinridge created the Frontier Nursing Service to bring family healthcare to some of the poorest, most isolated Appalachian families. In 1929, she imported her own English nurse-midwives, who set off on horseback to help deliver those babies.[14]

By 1970, training and qualifications for nurse-midwives had been standardized across the country, and their numbers began to explode. But to this day, they continue to fight for respect and recognition, a battle waged against hospitals, medical lobbying groups, and insurance companies for their right to practice independently, to be covered by Medicaid, and to qualify for liability insurance at rates that won't knock them right out of business.

And it all comes back to that tricky public-image issue. Even when a mom-to-be does her research and finds a midwife she is crazy about, there are plenty of doubters ready to second-guess her choice. Even in communities where counterculture, holistic feminism rules, you will find people whose ideals stop just short of putting their labor in the hands of a midwife. "I had no idea how radical it was not to use a doctor," says home-birth mom Caitlin. "I live in a part of Brooklyn that is very health-conscious and alternative. But when I took a prenatal yoga class and we went around the room to introduce ourselves and talk about our birth plans, I was absolutely shocked to discover that no one else was using a midwife."

Grandparents and parents are consistently stunned that their granddaughter or daughter would deliberately choose to use a low-tech midwife—an option they associate with *their* forebearers, who lived in an era before ultrasounds, antibiotics, and other lifesaving inventions. "My mom would only refer to my midwife as 'those people,' " says Nancy, who delivered her first child in a hospital. "Even after I carefully described her training and qualifications, she would call me up after a prenatal appointment and say, 'So, what did your doctor have to say?' "

Even if some people are scandalized by the idea of a midwife and others assume that they are mysterious women with candles and potions who flourished around the time of King Arthur, at least everyone's heard of the word. Now go ahead and ask your average, nonpregnant American citizen what a doula is, and be prepared for some very blank stares and some very strange answers:

*"It has something to do with babies, maybe a kind of diaper pail?"*

*"I heard a friend mention that word after she had just given birth, but I assumed she was still drugged up and speaking in tongues."*

*"I think it has something do with religion . . . something sexual or related to marriage. . . ."*

A few of the women I polled (none of whom were parents yet) had a vague idea that a doula helped in childbirth, but they basically assumed a midwife and a doula were inter-changeable. "Isn't it like a combination of midwife and baby nurse?" asked one woman, while another said, "My friend used one. It's someone who presides over a natural home birth." Two of the people I asked did have a clear defini-tion of what a doula actually does—but only because one worked at a women's health magazine and had written about alternative birth plans and the other had a room-mate who trained as a doula.

So here's what a birth doula does: She provides con-tinuous emotional and physi-cal support for a woman in labor. She will massage you,

## Do Doulas Really Help?

All that hand-holding, massaging, and encouragement can actually help you have an easier, shorter labor: A study in the *American Journal of Obstet-rics & Gynecology* found that women who had continuous doula support during labor reduced their chances of a C-section by 51 percent, reduced the odds of a forceps delivery by 57 per-cent, and reduced the length of their labor by more than an hour.[15]

talk you through contractions, fix you a snack, suggest dif-ferent laboring positions, help you pack up and get to the hospital, talk your shell-shocked partner through the expe-rience, and discuss your birth goals beforehand so she can speak up for you when you're too tired or dazed to do it your-self. In fact, any woman who has gone through childbirth herself and will stay by your side through your entire labor can act as your doula—your best friend, your sister, even your hairdresser if the two of you happen to be really close.

But here is where midwives and doulas are drastically different: Midwives deliver babies. Doulas do not. Midwives perform clinical tasks, such as listening to the baby's heartbeat, taking blood, even writing prescriptions for pain medications in some states. Doulas do not even take your temperature. Midwives train for years before they are qualified to practice. To become certified by the Doulas of North America, you need to take a sixteen-hour course, read five books from an approved reading list, and provide continuous support during three births[16]—so if you have a lot of pregnant friends due around the same time, it is possible to qualify in a fairly short time.

When you hire a doula, her entire focus is on making you comfortable. In fact, the word "doula" is Greek for "female slave." When I first heard about doulas, around the time I became pregnant with my first child, I fixated on the fact that it would be one more person to annoy me in the delivery room. I love my female friends, but I am certain if any of them had tried to tell me how to relax or rub my back during labor, I would have hissed at them like Linda Blair in *The Exorcist* before telling them to get the hell out of my room. That's basically what I did to my husband (at least until I got my epidural), and *he's* my favorite grownup in the world. So would I have wanted someone I barely knew whispering mantras in my ear? I didn't think so.

Caroline, a mother of one in Brooklyn, started out with a very similar attitude but found that a doula was exactly what she needed to get through her first birth: "I was completely skeptical," she recalls. "I am not a touchy-feely person at all. But as I got closer and closer to my due date, I started freaking out about everything—especially how I was going to get to the hospital, which was an hour away. I was crying to a friend over the phone, and she said, 'You have got to talk to my doula.' I was hesitant, since it was $1,500— a huge expense for us—but I agreed to meet her. And you know what? She really calmed me down. She described the whole process, and how she would know when to get me to the hospital, and that helped me regain a sense of control.

"My water broke three days after we had our first meeting. She came right over and we had tea while my husband went to get sandwiches and bring the car around. Every time I had a contraction, she pressed her hand down between my tailbone and waist and calmly talked me through it. If it had been my husband, I would have said, 'You freak, get your hands off me!' She knew I was an athlete, so in the car ride to the hospital—which took *forever*—she asked me to think about how I'd gotten through some tough times before, and I was able to focus on that. When we finally got to the hospital, I was already seven centimeters dilated, and I asked for the epidural. The doctor said, 'Oh, since you had a doula we thought you were going natural.' Ugh! But I got the epidural, and a couple of hours later I had the baby, with my doula cheering me on and my husband crying."

While a birth doula was not the right thing for me, I do think they are a great idea for women who can afford it and want a friendly, supportive presence in the room. Husbands and partners are irreplaceable, of course, but many retreat into an exhausted, ineffectual daze when the going gets tough. Doulas are especially helpful as advocates for women who are adamant about natural birth but are delivering in a hospital with an OB—though there is no guarantee the hospital staff will treat a doula with respect or listen to what she has to say.

And though this book is about childbirth, not parenthood or breastfeeding, I will digress for a moment to tell you how thrilled I was with my postpartum doula. During labor I reverted to some sort of primal, animalistic state, sitting alone in the dark, grunting and wincing, ready to bite off the head of anyone who came near me. But as soon as it was over and I made the transition from pregnancy to motherhood, all of a sudden I wanted as many women surrounding me as possible (everyone except that surly maternity-ward nurse who told me if it hurt when I was nursing, I must be doing it wrong). The day I came home from the hospital, I cried to my friend Katie, veteran breastfeeder of two daughters, that it felt like a metal clamp was snapping down on my nipples every time Bellamy attempted to nurse.

"Let me call my doula," she said.

Within an hour, Lori appeared at my door in a floppy hat, carrying a battered tote bag, sort of like a Mary Poppins for nursing mothers. With a big smile and a singsongy voice, she rearranged the pillows on my armchair, rubbed my feet, put up a pot of herbal tea, and observed my feeble attempts to breastfeed. "Well, no wonder it hurts. You need breast shields," she announced cheerfully. She hustled my husband off to the baby superstore, where she helped him load up on breast shields, bottle brushes, nursing pads, ointment, and all those other things that you never knew existed until you had a baby.

By the time Lori left that afternoon, I could actually nurse my baby without feeling like I was going through some painful S&M ritual. She visited a few more times and came back again after I had my second child. I have handed out her number to several of my friends, saying, "Oh, man, you have *got* to use a doula when you get home."

One good thing about a birth doula is that no one's really going to give you too much grief for hiring one. Oh, they may tease you for spending money on what they see as a glorified baby sitter ("Hey, give me a thousand bucks and I'll rub your back and play Enya for you!"), and your mom may be insulted that you didn't ask *her* to hang out with you in the delivery room, but basically they are seen as harmless cheerleaders, and since they are not actually delivering the baby, they pretty much fly under the radar of nosy, critical friends and relatives.

Besides, if anyone questions why you would hire a doula, you can always ask if *they* would be willing to stay up with you for hours on end, putting their needs aside to cater to your every need. "I am convinced that the most important thing that helped me give birth twice without pain relief was the support from my doula," says two-time home-birther Beth.

"My husband was great, but he had his own issues to deal with. The second time I gave birth it took more than thirty hours. I remember feeling overwhelmed in the middle of the night, thinking, *When the hell is this thing going to end?* But she stayed right there with me, holding my hand and saying, 'You're doing great, keep going, it's moving along.' And that's what got me through."

## CHAPTER SIX

# DRUG-FREE *in a* HIGH-TECH ZONE: NATURAL BIRTH *in a* HOSPITAL

*When I was in college, an older cousin who I really looked up to gave birth to her daughter at home. She was passionate about the fact that birth shouldn't be a medicalized, and she was so happy with her experience that I always had in the back of my mind that that was the best way to go. When I became pregnant, I wanted to go natural, but I ruled out home birth pretty quickly, since I'm just not that big a risk-taker. I looked into a birth center, but I was nervous about the fact that you have to leave after twenty-four hours, and I also have a medical condition that required an MD to oversee my birth, so I found an OB practice that was supportive of natural birth. I knew there were certain rules at the hospital I just couldn't get around: You have to get hooked up to an IV when you arrive, and after the delivery, they insist on giving you Pitocin to help shrink your uterus. I didn't like it, but I accepted it.*

*My water broke at 7:00 AM. I was pretty calm about it, and I didn't even call the doctor until 10:00 AM. I wanted to labor at home as long as possible, and I was only having mild contractions, so I propped myself up on the couch and worked on my laptop until around 3:00 PM. Finally, at 7:00 that evening, my doctor asked me to come in to the hospital because it had been twelve hours since my water broke. When I went in, I was only at one centimeter.*

*It turned out to be a very busy night for deliveries. When I arrived, there were no rooms available, so first I sat in a chair in a break room for two hours, which was very uncomfortable. Then I was moved to a glorified closet next to a room where someone else was giving birth. My labor had gotten very intense at that point. I was trying to walk around and getting pissed off every time a nurse came in to get supplies. I had studied the Bradley Method, but for that to work, I had to be in a calm environment with dim lights. The only good thing was that they left me alone. I wasn't forced to get the IV and antibiotics until I was put in a delivery room three hours after I arrived.*

*Once I was in the room, my husband rubbed my back and played music, and we tried a lot of the meditation stuff we had learned in our Bradley class. I was prepared for the pain, but it was a lot more intense than I had anticipated. I had this vision that I was going to be able to lie there and get into full relaxation. But I needed to be on my feet, walking around, squatting, rocking on my hands and knees, and vocalizing. At one point I said to my husband, 'What was I thinking? I can't do this!' And he said, 'Oh, good, if it hurts that much, it must mean you're in transition.' Sure enough, I was at nine centimeters and almost ready to push. The pushing was much easier than the pain up to that point. I pushed for a good two hours. I didn't want anyone counting out loud for me—that was too in-my-face—so I just pushed as long as I felt comfortable. My doctor was supportive; she never threatened to go in with the forceps or anything. Nathan was born at 5:00 AM. It was a long ordeal, and I was exhausted, but I have to say I felt pretty elated. I was really proud that I was able to do it naturally.*

**DEBRA, STAY-AT-HOME MOTHER OF THREE**
*Lewisburg, Pennsylvania*

Debra and I met in the mid-'90s through that tangled network of childhood friends, college roommates, and other assorted acquaintances that makes up your social life before you have kids. Though we never hung out one-on-one, I always felt a kind of kinship with her—we're both products of suburban Jewish upbringings in the '70s, and both love books, so we both wound up working in publishing. She even dated my brother before she married another old friend of mine. Then one day in the early summer of 2001, when we were both hugely pregnant and munching on burgers at a friend's backyard barbeque, we discovered that we had one other thing in common: We were both planning on delivering our babies at the very same hospital with the very same doctor.

But even though the backdrop and cast of supporting characters were going to be almost identical for our deliveries, our attitudes toward the big event could not have been more different. I had already grilled my doctor about how long she would make me wait before giving me an epidural ("Can I have one now?" I joked at my eight-month checkup). Debra, on the other hand, was convinced that she could use relaxation techniques she learned in a Bradley class to get through her labor, without the help of drugs.

I smiled at her as she told me this, with one thought crashing through my head: *Is she out of her freakin' mind?*

You wouldn't try to *om* yourself into a state of relaxation for an appendectomy, I reasoned, so why on earth would you try that for something as painful as childbirth? Why suffer through *any* kind of intense pain when modern medical science says you don't have to? What was she trying to prove?

This disconnect, this inability to even fathom why someone would go through such a grueling ordeal without so much as a shot of gin, is, I found, a pretty common reaction when mainstream, medicated-childbirth moms are confronted with anyone who mentions natural childbirth. While some do have a grudging admiration for these women and say they might have tried it if they were a little less squeamish about pain, many of the moms I spoke to believe that the motivating factor for childbirth without drugs is a unique and very irritating form of female machismo.

"If you're going to go to the effort of being in a hospital, rather than at home or in a whirlpool somewhere, you might as well take advantage of the drugs!" said a mother of two whose second child was delivered by C-section. "They don't hand out a prize at the end saying 'World's Best Mom.' I think these women are very self-righteous about the whole thing."

The more I talked to moms on both sides of the debate, the more I began to see that so-called natural moms and medicated moms are like two separate tribes standing on either side of a great big, gaping canyon: Each group is looking across, shaking their heads, suspicious of the other, but unable to get close enough to hear what they are saying. So instead of making the effort to understand each other, we just grab onto our first impression and stay with it.

In fact, while researching this book, I attended a hospital seminar on pain-management options for laboring women. One of the women there had a question about less invasive medical alternatives to spinals and epidurals, but she prefaced her comment by saying, "Not that I'm one of those crazy religious fanatics who wants 'natural birth' . . . " As everyone else in the room laughed in agreement, I realized that for some medicated-birth women, the idea of foregoing an epidural during labor is lumped into the same category as shunning vaccines or saying "no" to blood transfusions. This is not a logical choice, they think, but a fundamentalist, reactionary, and uneducated one—the women who choose this option are forsaking science; they are turning their backs on good old common sense, all for some misguided notion that being a martyr for your baby somehow makes you a superior mother.

And the natural-birth moms look back across that great big divide and say, *Bullshit.*

"First of all, choosing natural childbirth does not necessarily mean choosing pain," Noemi, a Brooklyn mom-to-be told me in a long, passionate email. "It's not like we don't worry about the pain—there's no question we have all heard the horror stories from all the women who faithfully impart the gospel of the outrageous pain of labor to anyone with the slightest belly. It's the possibility of it being *manageable* that you usually don't hear about." Noemi had spoken to numerous natural-birth veterans and was convinced that with vigorous preparation, she would be able to control her pain—and perhaps even eliminate it entirely.

## Can You Psych Yourself out of Pain?

In the patented HypnoBirthing method of preparing for childbirth, moms-to-be use breathing and visualization to achieve a completely relaxed state during labor. Does it work? A 2004 meta-analysis in the *British Journal of Anaesthesia* found that when women used hypnosis, they were less likely to require epidurals or other painkillers during labor.[1]

I wished her the best of luck, but remained somewhat doubtful that a *completely* pain-free birth could be achieved without any anesthesia. In fact, of the nearly fifty natural-birth moms I spoke with, I could only find one who claimed that her labor was "delightful." Several described it as "empowering" or "manageable," and one or two said, "It was more like intense discomfort than pain." But the majority admitted, "Of course there was pain! It hurt like hell!" Through concentration, movement, vocalizing, massage, and other methods, however, they felt they were able to dial it down just enough to make it through to the end without drugs.

While listening to some of these descriptions, I started wondering, were the actual *physical* sensations of labor different for these women than they were for me, or did they simply process the pain differently? Was there some miraculous quirk of their physiology or a secret hormone only they produced that converted what I felt as sheer agony into "manageable discomfort"?

Maybe some women do have a much easier time with labor—just as every woman's body is different, the details of every pregnancy are different. Some women labor for twenty-one hours, some for ninety minutes (I personally experienced both extremes). Babies are positioned differently in the womb, and even full-term babies can range in size from five-pound peanuts to ten-pound baby Buddhas. For my first pregnancy, the contractions felt like a steel vise clamping around my back; for my second pregnancy, they felt like the world's worst gas pains. Other moms have described the pain as anything from "a set of knives piercing my lower back" to "an ocean wave coming and going" to "really, really bad period cramps" to "severe constipation."

*How much pain?* I would ask. *Can you quantify it?* But after many months of prodding women to describe their physical experience of labor, I realized that trying to get an accurate gauge of other people's pain was pretty fruitless. It's like describing the color blue. You can use all the adjectives you can find in your pocket thesaurus, but no one can ever know exactly what it is you are seeing or feeling unless they are inside your brain.

But let's say we assumed the physical constriction of the uterine muscles and all the accompanying side effects were exactly the same for each woman. Still, how each woman mentally processes this pain is quite different—a process determined by everything from your emotional reaction to labor to your mental and physical preparation for it to your entire personal history with pain, discomfort, hardship, and endurance. "I believe that pain starts in the mind," explained Laurie, who was so empowered by her two holistic births that she now teaches natural-childbirth classes. "The minute your body goes into fear mode, the blood vessels close down, the good hormones stop, and the bad hormones start. And the more pain you feel, the more scared you get, so it's a nasty cycle." I will never believe anyone who claims that childbirth is not inherently painful—after all, your muscles are constricting strongly enough to push a full-term baby out—but the idea that the pattern and intensity of the pain are influenced by your reaction to it does make a lot of sense.

One thing is certain: No matter what these moms were feeling —lapping waves of discomfort or crashing tsunamis of pain—they all agreed that the natural pain of contractions was far less awful to contemplate than a needle full of chemicals injected into their spines.

Several women simply said they hated needles of any kind, especially a long one that was going into such a sensitive area (many of these same women resisted having a standard IV put in their arm and chose not to go through amniocentesis). Fair enough. But even more disconcerting than the painful prick of a needle was what is *in* that needle (a combination of a local anesthetic and a narcotic). Now, you can find countless articles with titles like "The Epidural Epidemic" that enumerate the potential dangers of obstetric anesthesia,[2] and you can find plenty of studies that say the side effects of current low-dose epidurals are minor and insignificant[3]—until I get my doctorate in scientific analysis, I will not presume to know the truth. But I have to say, wherever the truth lies about the acute or long-term effects of an epidural, at least these women are consistent about questioning every single substance that goes into their bodies. Every pregnant woman I have ever talked to, no matter the circumstances of her delivery, will say she was at least somewhat more vigilant about her health and diet during her pregnancy—cutting back on alcohol, caffeine, swordfish, and sushi, for instance—but on the last day, as we approach the finish line, more than half of us wind up saying to our doctors, "Go ahead, bring on the drugs."

Among natural-birth moms, there is a fierce sense of skepticism that, no matter what the FDA and the American College of Obstetricians and Gynecologists say, you can never be 100 percent sure of the effects of any foreign substance you put in your body. "I'm asthmatic and allergic to practically everything on the planet," explained Susan, a mother of two in Upper Montclair, New Jersey. "I've always had a severe reaction to the most innocent things—I'll hyperventilate and break out in hives. So you know what? It just wasn't worth it to me to put something new into my system."

And you don't have to have had any unfortunate runins with drugs (legal or not) to be wary about introducing a chemical into your nervous system that will shift the locus of control from the inside your body to the outside. For women who have put their faith in the mind-body connection, the idea of shutting the brain off from what is going on below the waist is creepy and unacceptable. "I had heard that the epidural can make both your delivery and your recovery longer," said Sheila, an ecologist in Tucson, Arizona, who delivered in a hospital with an OB and a doula. "And I hated the idea that I would feel unconnected to my body. I wanted to have the full experience of childbirth without dulled senses."

Even more powerful than the fear of what the epidural will do to one's body is the fear of what it will do to the baby. "I've done all the research, and I'm convinced that natural childbirth is just safer," said Claudia, a mom in North Salem, New York, who delivered two babies naturally. "The drugs *do* affect your baby. I read one study that said that babies who are exposed to drugs during labor have a greater chance of growing up to be drug abusers later in life. Who knows if it's true or not? But at least it's one less thing I have to worry about." Other moms believed that the baby would be more alert and more eager to breastfeed after a drug-free birth.

A few women argued that, even though epidurals are accepted by the medical establishment today, you never know what will come up in the future. "I didn't want to do anything that even had the remote possibility of hurting my baby," said Zywia, a mom in Wappingers Falls, New York, who gave birth to her three children in the 1980s. "When I was a little girl, I saw all those pictures of Thalidomide babies, and it left the impression on me that we have to be extremely careful of what we put in our bodies during pregnancy."

Look, it's simple, these women told me: If it is possible to manage the pain in ways that have zero chance of negatively affecting the baby— talking, breathing, hypnosis, taking a hot shower, grunting, listening to a favorite Brahms symphony—why on earth choose something that has even a *theoretical* possibility of causing harm?

"I really thought it was the best choice for myself and my child," Ruby, a mother of two in Portland, Maine, told me. "No one's ever going to prove how things affect the child when it's born, whether babies can really remember the circumstance of their birth. But in my heart I felt like I wanted my children born in the most wholesome, nurturing way."

In many of the most fundamental ways, the women I met who delivered naturally in a hospital were indistinguishable from their counterparts who delivered at home or in a birth center. They, too, questioned the motives of medical doctors and were put off by their perceived arrogance. They tended to lead more "natural" lifestyles, shopping in organic markets, embracing holistic medicine, laying off excessive amounts of caffeine or alcohol. I got a pretty strong vibe that Pop-Tarts and Cheetos would not be appearing in their kids' lunch boxes.

They put a high value on endurance and had most likely spent their entire pregnancies—if not their entire adult lives—mentally and physically preparing for the marathon of childbirth. There were runners, hikers, and yoginis; there were women who get up at the crack of dawn and trek through snowstorms to make their daily appointment at the gym. "I've run two marathons, and I know my training and daily running helped me tremendously in preparing for birth," said Sheila. "I was actually able to use many of the endurance techniques to help me through labor."

They make a clear distinction between negative pain (your body's alarm system telling you something is wrong that needs to be fixed) and positive pain (part of normal bodily functions telling you everything is working just fine). One woman told me that while she had no problem popping a Tylenol when she had a headache, it would never even occur to her to take medicine for her menstrual cramps.

I think one of the key reasons all these women—ones who delivered at home, at a birth center, or in a hospital— were able to get through labor *au naturel* was that they had developed a preternatural ability to see past the moment and have a broader perspective of just where childbirth pain fits in the grand scheme of things. When I was in the throes of labor, I could not visualize even sixty seconds into the future. Each contraction swallowed me whole, and the pain was the beginning and end of my sense of self. The only thought in my head was how to get through the pain or—better yet—put an end to it. But somehow, through it all, these women are able to focus on the fact that as murky and distant as it may seem, there actually *is* an end to the pain. "The thing about labor is that the pain is fleeting," said Susan. "It's not like you're in bed for six months with a terrifying disease and you're throwing up the whole time. Labor is several hours of something very, very intense, and then it's over. As soon as the baby is out, the pain is gone."

But here's a question: If everything about their philosophy says gentle birth, drug-free birth, no interventions, no medical interference, why would these women willingly walk through the doors of a hospital, with all its machines, needles, and drugs? Most of these moms stressed that while they supported the idea of home birth and birth centers, the perceived safety of the hospital simply overrode any other consideration. After weighing the negatives of standardized medical care against the security of having emergency systems in place for just-in-case scenarios, the hospital won out. Some of the women I interviewed for this chapter confirmed that they had mulled over the possibility of a home birth but dismissed it as too risky or too difficult to sell to their nonbelieving families.

"The most important thing for me was to have a midwife,

because I wanted a holistic approach to childbirth, but I still liked the idea of having a medical setting surrounding me in case something went wrong," explained Dawn, a public-relations director and mother of two in Oak Park, Illinois. "I found a group of midwives who deliver out of a hospital with an alternative birth center, and that seemed like the perfect situation. With my first birth, my blood pressure spiked after four hours of labor, so I was moved to the regular unit, where I immediately asked for an epidural—which I later regretted. The second time, I switched to a different birth center at a different hospital, and it was a completely different atmosphere. It was set up more like a bedroom than a hospital, with a double bed and a Jacuzzi. I was required to go through triage, but when they checked me, I was already at seven centimeters, so they just brought me into the birthing center, and I delivered in the tub a few minutes later."

Many women simply did not have the option of an independent birth center: "My husband had always dreamed of his wife giving birth in the water, but in Corpus Christi, Texas, that just was not an option," explained Barbara, a stay-at-home mother of two. And then there are the quirky, but no less important, logistical reasons for heading to the hospital: "I live in an apartment building, and I just didn't want to have to worry about how much noise I was making!" explained Carrie, a mother of one in Los Angeles. "Besides, my mom was barely coping with the idea that I was using a midwife instead of a doctor, so if I went out of the hospital, she would have totally freaked out."

While the most outspoken home-birth and natural-birth advocates contend that doctors are always looking for an excuse to intervene and try out their shiny new surgical tools, all the obstetricians I spoke to for this book said they were happiest when a patient had an uncomplicated, spontaneous vaginal delivery. And though a doctor will suggest an epidural if the mother seems to be exhausted or in extraordinary pain, no one is going to flip you over and jab a needle in your back against your will.

Still, though low-intervention births may be the ideal, hospitals are designed for maximum efficiency, and they require standards and protocols to keep things moving along and to avoid the possibility of malpractice suits. Many hospitals require you to have an IV in your arm and an electronic fetal monitor strapped around your waist—which will severely curtail your ability to get up and walk around. You will almost certainly be "on the clock," and if your labor isn't progressing in a timely manner, get ready to be eased along with Pitocin. Because a hospital has a finite number of resources, including delivery rooms, nurses, and doctors, and a much larger volume of births than a birth center (a hospital may see a dozen babies born each night, whereas a birth center will have only one or two), it is highly unlikely that they will say, "Take your time, no rush, we have all night" if there are three other moms cooling their heels in the waiting room.

The consensus among the moms I interviewed is that the most supportive hospital setting for completing a natural labor is to use a midwife at an in-hospital birth center, if you have that option available to you. Some of these so-called birth centers are basically standard labor-and-delivery rooms with a few extra dollars in the decorating budget for prettier sheets on the bed, a few paintings on the walls, and a birthing ball in the corner. They still may require standard hospital interventions (after all, natural birth isn't just about not using anesthesia, it's about resisting all unnatural interference, such as induction, episiotomy, and vacuum- or forceps-assisted delivery). Critics claim these rooms are nothing more than a marketing ploy intended to attract women who are looking for a different birth experience without actually providing one.

But there are other birthing centers within hospitals that are closer to the American Association of Birth Centers's ideal of a noninvasive birth (though only a handful of these have been found low-tech enough to earn official AABC recognition). These centers tend to have primary care by midwives, with MDs on call as a backup, and a few even allow water birth. Still, since it is within a hospital, you will most likely be required to go through triage, which means having an internal exam and at least temporarily being put on a monitor to see how far your labor has progressed.

But not all hospitals have such cozy, supportive birth centers, and some women, despite it all, still want the security of having a medical doctor deliver their baby (or in some cases, they have medical concerns, such as asthma, hyper-thyroidism, or preeclampsia, that require more medical oversight). So a woman desiring a natural birth might find herself right there in the labor and delivery ward, surrounded by women who are eager for medicated pain relief and nurses and interns who look at them quizzically when they say, "Thanks, but no thanks."

And there is the catch. Giving birth in a hospital provides you with that highly valued safety net, but tagging along with that net is a sly little devil called Temptation. For no matter how much you set your mind to the viability and beauty of a drug-free birth, if you deliver in a hospital, there will always be some corner of your brain that knows the drugs are there. Somewhere down those Linoleum-tiled hallways, lurking in a supply closet or on another floor, there is a man or woman holding a needle who can make your pain disappear: All you have to do is ask. And this is where the natural-hospital moms I interviewed split off into two philosophically different groups. While there was a contingent of moms who chose to deliver in a hospital partly because they *didn't* want to rule out the option of painkillers, others looked at their presence as dangerous and unnecessary, ready to suck you in at your lowest, most vulnerable point. "Natural seems to be the goal for so many health-conscious, freethinking, liberal-minded mothers, and it certainly was for me," said Amy, an entrepreneur and mother of two in New York. "But when you're that close to pain relief, as I was, it is hard, if not impossible, to abstain. I wound up asking for an epidural both times."

And while some of the women were so disappointed

and angry with themselves for giving in that they chose a home birth or birth center birth for their next pregnancy, others couldn't say enough about how grateful they were that they had the option to partake. "I had incredibly painful back labor," said Jeanne, a New York costume designer who labored in a hospital birthing center with a midwife. "After twenty hours, I was so exhausted, I couldn't even listen to what the midwife was saying. So I finally said, 'I've had enough, I want to go upstairs and get an epidural.' I ran into the elevator with my butt hanging out of my gown and got myself up to the labor ward as quickly as I could. When I got the epidural, I was finally able to rest for a half hour, which was unbelievably great; it was just the bit of relief I needed. When I woke up, I was able to listen to the midwife and focus, and I pushed Tyler out in a half hour."

Of course, after you've spent months telling everyone how eager you are to have a natural birth, they might not actually listen when you ask for the drugs, as Jeanne discovered. "When I first asked for the epidural, my midwife said, 'I don't believe you, I know you really want to do this!' I was in terrible pain, and here I was arguing with her. Finally, my husband pulled my midwife aside and said, 'I know she really wants it, so please give it to her.' "

Many women prepare for this by putting plans in place, creating code words. One popular strategy is, "If I ask for it once, ignore me; if I ask for it twice, I mean it." Dawn, like many of the women I spoke with, had encouraged her husband to try to talk her out of it. "I also worked out certain catchphrases with my midwife: If I said one thing, then she had to say, 'No, we're not going to do it.' But there was one special word that meant *I'm not kidding anymore.*"

The most challenging aspect of natural birth for so many of these moms isn't dealing with the pain, it's dealing with all the nonbelievers who say things like, "Oh, honey, that's so cute that you think you can do it without drugs! But believe me, when those contractions really kick in, you are going to be screaming just as loudly as I did for the epidural."

Well, at least they're not accusing you of reckless endangerment.

Moms who choose the natural-in-a-hospital option do have the benefit of bypassing the most severe criticisms that slam out-of-hospital moms. ("You're risking your life! You're risking your baby's life! What if there's an emergency?!") What they get instead is a patronizing pat on the head: "My mother kept saying, 'You've got to get the saddle block,' which I think is what they called the epidural back in her day. I finally had to just tune her out," said Nina, a mother of two in Indianapolis. "But I got the most grief from a friend who is an OB. She kept calling me up with lists of

*"Childbirth always seems to be depicted the same in the media: screaming during labor and crying after the delivery and maybe some demands for drugs. That just wasn't my experience. I may have had a pained look on my face, but I stayed calm, and I never screamed—I just asked for music, popsicles, wet rags, and status reports."*

other drugs I could take if I didn't want the epidural. It's as if no one believed I could really do it."

Been-there-done-that moms often listen to your plans and then go off on their own reverie of how fabulous their epidural was. One woman's mother tried to convince her to give up her natural plans and just go ahead and schedule a C-section, as she had with all three of her own children. A hospital-based natural birth is looked at as a harmless, childlike fantasy: *That's right, dear, you go and try to dig that tunnel to China in the backyard with a toy shovel and a Dixie cup.*

And for women who are spending megawatts of mental energy pumping themselves up for their impending drug-free birth, this can be not only annoying, but intrusive and hurtful. "My parents and in-laws were concerned that we were 'too set' on natural childbirth, and that I'd be hard on myself if it didn't work out," said Amanda, a lawyer in Burlington, Vermont. "In retrospect, I can see their point, though at the time it was really offensive to me. My whole method of preparation was envisioning that it *was* possible. I was worried that if they made me doubt myself the tiniest bit, it would have a domino effect, and I needed to be in a completely positive frame of mind."

And it's not just friends and family who question your ability to go the whole nine yards. Some women recalled both doctors and nurses who came in to check on them every hour or so to ask, "Change your mind yet?" And even though many women choose midwives specifically to support a hands-off, natural labor, one mom told me her midwife spent an entire week pressuring her to induce her labor; another was disturbed that her midwife insisted on manually breaking her water. "I saw a rotating group of midwives in the practice, and the one who wound up doing my delivery was the one I felt the least comfortable with," recalled Emily, a writer in Amherst, Massachusetts. "When my labor was taking some time to get going in the beginning, she suggested Pitocin right away, and I said, 'Well, can't we try nipple stimulation instead?' I was surprised she would suggest something so mainstream when there were natural alternatives we hadn't even tried yet."

So you're in the hospital. You've got the proximity of pain-relief medication there to tempt you, and you may have a mother or a grandma or a nurse or a best friend (either in the room or in your head) telling you, "It's okay, go ahead, drugs are your friend. . . ." How do you keep it together and focus on your goal of natural birth?

The key is in the preparation. If you're not going to deliver in a setting that is designed specifically to encourage natural birth, you have to make sure your little corner of the hospital is as conducive as possible to staying drug- and intervention-free. The first and most important step is to find a midwife or doctor who is completely supportive of your birth plan. Don't just assume the ob-gyn who you've known since you were sixteen will be cool with your plan to deliver naturally. Grill him or her about induction, episiotomy, and

C-section rates, and don't be afraid to switch practitioners in the middle of your pregnancy if you're not happy with their answers (or, more important, with their attitude).

And don't forget that in a hospital, you will spend many more hours with nurses than with your doctor, so find out all the protocols and have your doctor call in specific instructions to override them if possible (she will have to let the nursing staff know if she will allow you to eat or have intermittent monitoring, for example). "I interviewed two midwife practices and toured two different hospitals, and I compared the C-section and episiotomy rates," says Emily. "We chose the hospital that was smaller, farther away, and had less fancy equipment, because we liked the low-key feel there so much more."

Other moms who delivered their children in more than one hospital agreed that the smaller the hospital, the less intrusive the staff—and statistics bear this out. The fewer the number of beds in the maternity ward, the lower the rate of epidurals. (This can be attributed to the fact that lower-volume institutions might not have an obstetric anesthesiologist on duty 24/7.)[4]

Once you have your doctor or midwife set, get to work assembling your support team. Because though you may be the one doing all the hard work, a natural birth really is a team effort. It takes perseverance, the powers of persuasion, and a rock-solid ability to stand your ground in the face of opposition. And even if you possess these qualities in abundance in your everyday life, who's to say what you will be capable of when you are in pain or in deep concentration and barely able to speak? Every one of the women I interviewed had a partner or a doula who was prepped to fight for her right to labor naturally when her labor got too intense for her to speak for herself.

"Throughout the birth my husband really knew what he was doing," recalls Kendra, a mother of three in St. Louis. "He spoke to the doctors for me and helped out with anything I needed. We had practiced what he would say in different situations. I really don't think you can have a long labor where you're trying to go natural without someone to support you."

The moms who were the most successful at avoiding any drugs or interventions were the ones who had done the most prep work. So, as soon as you get an

*"I felt like I was back in college and everyone was saying, 'Come on, just take one hit from the bong.' That made me dig in my heels even more and say, 'Look, I do not want to have an epidural!' "*

inkling that natural birth is the best choice for you, it's best to start gearing up both mentally and physically. Sign up for a natural-childbirth class such as Bradley or Lamaze (the "preparing for childbirth" classes offered by hospitals are generally useless), check out those prenatal yoga tapes, read up on your options, and talk to other women who have successfully given birth naturally. But don't wait until week thirty-nine. "Childbirth is like an athletic event you have to train for," says Noemi. "I mean, if I tried to run a marathon tomorrow, it would be really painful and I would fail miserably. A lot of times you watch those childbirth reality shows and someone says, 'I'm going to have a natural birth!' but they haven't done any preparation at all, so they get to the hospital and lie down on their back for fourteen hours, and they're in pain and they're terrified. You have to exercise and train and do everything you can to make sure it goes well—that's the only way you have a chance of succeeding."

## A Playlist for Labor

Among the music recommended by *Deliver This!* moms to help you focus:

Peter Gabriel

Hank Williams, Jr.

anything electronic

Marilyn Manson ("The hard stuff is good for the pain.")

Matthew Sweet

Roxy Music

Miriam Makeba

Show tunes

So now we know why women choose natural birth and how they do it. But let's get to that question that has been hovering over this discussion, the one that seems to push us all apart and fill the space in between with a toxic mix of anger and resentment: *Do moms who give birth naturally feel superior to moms who don't, or is that feeling all just our own insecurities being reflected back on us?*

Here's one thing I can tell you: Natural moms feel certain that they had a superior birth *experience*. They feel their labor was more empowering and fulfilling than the experience of women who spent their baby's birth day numb from the waist down. There is a unique brand of exhilaration, an outsize bliss that natural-birth moms say they feel. Yes, there is the same sense of relief that *any* new mom with a healthy baby experiences, and the same onrush of hormones that can present itself as overpowering love, a surge of fierce maternal protectiveness, or even a mess of irrational tears. But then add to that already-potent emotional mix the sense of achievement at having pushed yourself past the finish line on your own terms (plus a satisfying kick of "I told you so" to all the people who said you couldn't do it), and you're going to get a kind of jubilation that is easily misinterpreted as a smug sense of superiority.

But I don't think that's all of it. Many of the medicated moms I interviewed said they suspected the natural moms believe that their birth choice makes them better mothers. "I know," sighed many of the natural moms when I ran this idea by them. "Believe me, I don't think I'm a superwoman," said Kendra. "I don't think I'm a better mother than you. But I know people think that. They may not say it right to your face, but they are definitely thinking it."

And how could they not, when so many natural moms say their motivating factor is doing what is "best for the child"? Read between the lines, and that means that if you choose a different path, you are putting your own need for pain relief ahead of the health of your unborn baby. You are saying that dealing with a few hours of discomfort is too high a price to pay to give your baby the best possible start in the world.

I cannot presume to know what's going on in the mind of every woman who chooses natural birth. Are there some out there who truly believe they are better, more self-sacrificing moms than everyone else? Of course. But you can find women on every point of the childbirth-choices continuum who would say the same thing about themselves.

Natural-birth moms know that this is an issue, and several told me they worried that the resentment surrounding the "better-mom superiority complex" could create a backlash. In fact, many told me they cautiously played down their own excitement about their birth experience so it would not be misinterpreted as a judgment on someone else's choice. "I rarely say anything about my birth story, mostly because it's such a touchy subject and I don't know how to do it without opening the floodgates," admitted Emily. "I have all this information that I want to share with other mothers, but how can I do it without sounding like a harridan? Really, all I want to do is let people know there is another option to the standard medical birth. I don't want them to think I'm judging them as mothers."

If there is one area where natural-birth moms are admittedly judgmental, it is in their belief that medicated moms have not done their homework; that they have blindly accepted the standard model of interventions and epidurals without even considering the implications. "They think we're crazy for choosing natural, but we think *they're* crazy for just going along with whatever their doctor orders," admitted Debra.

There is a sense of sadness, a feeling that far too many women are missing out on nature's greatest experience, and bewilderment about why so many moms would choose to surrender their sensations before they even got a sense of how far they could go. "I think it's a little sad that women don't even want to try it," said Claudia. "I learned something really powerful about myself when I gave birth naturally. I thought I was a wuss, but I found I had more strength than I ever imagined."

"I think women are prouder when they have natural childbirth; it's a nice accomplishment to have," said Laurie. "I think if you buy into the marketing propaganda, things that are decided by hospitals and drug companies, then you're missing an amazing opportunity. It's like, hello, this is the closest to nature we get! This really is our core essence as women."

## CHAPTER SEVEN

# EPIDURAL BLISS: MEDICATED VAGINAL BIRTH *in a* HOSPITAL

*When I was pregnant with my first child, I was finishing up my medical residency in Chicago while my husband was living in St. Louis. I moved down to St. Louis four weeks before my due date, and then I was like, "Okay, I'm ready, where's the baby?" After my thirty-eight-week checkup, I went home and defrosted the refrigerator, and that night I woke up around 2:30 AM with contractions. I had so much adrenaline that they didn't even bother me at first.*

*We hung around for a while, but at 5:00 AM they were five minutes apart, so we went to the hospital. That's when the contractions really started hurting, and I had trouble even walking. The nurses in triage checked me, and I was already six centimeters dilated. They said, "Are you sure you want an epidural? You're so close." And I said, "There's no way you can convince me the last four centimeters won't be even worse!" It wasn't until I got the epidural that I realized that every single muscle in my body had been tensed up and in pain—after, it was like I had taken a huge breath and all the tension was gone. It was an overwhelmingly relaxed feeling. I remember I did have a contraction while the anesthesiologist was administering the epidural, but the nurse talked me through it. There was just one brief little zing down the side of my leg from the needle, but really, the worst part was that the betadine they put on to sterilize my back was so cold!*

*I spent the next couple of hours reading some dopey magazine and listening to music; there was a surreal, expectant air to the whole thing. By 10:00 AM, I was ready to push. The doctor tried to wheel a mirror over so I could watch, and I said, "Just wheel that right back over to the other side of the room, thank you very much!" I pushed for around forty-five minutes—it never hurt, but I was definitely able to feel the pressure. My husband told me that when the baby was halfway out, he opened one eye and winked at everyone!*

*When I finally pushed him out, my husband cut the cord, they put him in a little towel, and I held him within a minute. I remember thinking,* Wow, he's my little miracle! *I was relieved it was over and things went so well, and overwhelmed that the thing I had waited for for so long had finally happened.*

**SHARON, PHYSICIAN AND MOTHER OF TWO**
*St. Louis, Missouri*

Now *that* is a story I can relate to.

After spending the better part of a year listening to moms

eloquently and passionately explain to me why they chose to go through childbirth without any drugs or any interventions, I absolutely understand why it was the best possible choice for them, and how it made their day of labor an incredible, empowering experience. I sit here in awe of their perseverance and willpower. And I think about everything I went through during my first labor—the Pitocin and the epidural, the catheter and the blood pressure cuff—and I realize that while it wasn't quite as beautiful and inspiring a scenario, it worked for me, and if I were to do it all over again, I would still choose a medicated vaginal hospital birth.

Mind you, it's not like my preference for medicated labor is based on nothing. I *did* experience natural labor for a good six or seven hours with my first daughter's birth. The first couple of hours after my water broke were definitely manageable—the contractions were mild as my husband and I walked around the darkened, hushed corridors of the labor and delivery ward, showing off my new leopard-print slippers to the night shift nurses and practicing how we were going to tell all our friends the story of my water breaking right after the crème brûlée had been cleared.

But by hours three and four, even though I had not yet had any interventions (other than the internal exam and monitoring during triage), I could not walk anymore. I could hardly breathe. I am amazed at the stories of women vigorously pacing, bouncing, and squatting during labor, because for me, the Herculean effort of moving my body even one tiny little inch was only rewarded by an invisible gremlin twisting a rusty steak knife even deeper into my back. When Jeremy made the fatal mistake of trying to help, I growled at him as if I were possessed by demons. The only thing I could possibly do was sit on the bed, staring at the clock and cursing the fact that an entire ice age could come and go in the time it took for the skinny hand to tick ahead one second. After an hour or so of helplessly watching this, Jeremy wisely retreated to a chair and fell asleep.

I have dug deep into my psyche and come to the conclusion that for me, there was nothing beautiful or empowering about my stint doing natural labor. The only thing I learned about myself was this: I really don't like extreme pain, and I have a previously unexplored capacity to be a nasty bitch when I'm experiencing it.

And yes, after talking to natural-birth moms, I do acknowledge that my perception of the pain could have been affected by listening to all those stories passed around our culture about the agonies of childbirth, and I'm sure my emotions were mucking about with my hormones. Perhaps if I had learned a relaxation method that was more useful than those ridiculous *hee-hee-hee* breaths that they teach in childbirth class (which, by the way, no one actually uses), I could have made it further along without anesthesia. But you know what? It just didn't matter that much to me. Achieving a powerful, organic birth experience was not as high up on my list of priorities as having a safe, comfortable delivery. And though I understand the other side of the argument, for *me* to feel safest, I needed to be in a hospital.

And for me to feel relaxed and comfortable, I needed to have an epidural.

Because I am someone who is blissfully immersed in mainstream media on a daily basis, I like and respect almost all of the doctors I know, and I believe that technology has made our lives better, not worse. I spent one miserable weekend getting in touch with nature by camping out near the Delaware River and swore never to do it again. I happily use medication for pain relief and think big-city hospitals are actually interesting, exciting places.

I had no interest in rewiring thirty-four years' worth of beliefs, interests, and experiences so I could get through labor naturally. Not only would that kind of birth plan require a fundamental change in my personal philosophy, it would also require months of preparation and training— and even if I had that time to spare, I could find about eight million other things I would rather do with it.

But on that summer day in 2001, as I sat in the labor ward of NYU Medical Center, none of this was going through my head. I was not thinking about mind-body connections or my personal feelings toward the medical profession. All I was thinking about was the unbearable pain I was going through, and the fact that there was a safe (according to the FDA and my doctor), proven method for making it stop. It was all about Dr. Fannypack.

After I spent a very unpleasant hour or so on Stadol, my doctor finally agreed to page the anesthesiologist. In walked the one of the dorkiest men I had ever seen (and believe me, as someone who has been to both *Star Trek* conventions and crossword-puzzle tournaments, I have definitely seen my share): He was wearing thick glasses with square frames that were way too big for his head, and his shoulders sloped forward in the manner of a teenager who has spent too many hours hunched over his *Dungeons & Dragons* books. From my vantage point at the end of my bed, eyes focused about waist-high, the one detail I fixated on was the green nylon fanny pack strapped around his middle. I may have been clenching every muscle in pain, but I was lucid enough to think that I hadn't seen a "fashion don't" like that since the time I got swallowed by a swarm of tourists on the Statue of Liberty ferry during a high school field trip.

But by that point, Dr. Fannypack was as magnetically appealing to me as Jude Law and Russell Crowe combined. After all, somewhere in that pack, and somewhere in his brain, were the tools and knowledge to make my pain go away. Jeremy woke up just in time to announce I was allergic to iodine, which added ten minutes to my torture as the nurse hunted down an alternative antiseptic. Finally, I leaned over the bed and got my epidural and my geeky hero slipped back into the night.

I don't remember feeling the needle go into my back. All I remember is that after one or two more contractions, the pain was gone. It was almost dawn, and the sun coming up outside my window was the perfect metaphor for the way my mood changed from darkness to delight. Before the epidural, I couldn't even look at Jeremy. Now, I was able to lie back peacefully and hold his hand while he read me the recap of the previous night's Mets game. I was able to relax, think about the baby, and shake off the mumbling, miserable persona I had unwillingly taken on. I reverted to my normal happy-go-lucky self—and *that* was the person whom I thought should greet my baby when she entered the world.

The price I paid for that transformation was that in the dozen more hours that I labored, I was subjected to a steady stream of interventions: Pitocin, an internal fetal monitor, a catheter. It's true that these interventions made me a prisoner of my hospital bed, but hey, I wasn't going anywhere anyway. I had the newspaper, my husband, a TV, a telephone. I was

---

**Packing 101**

Forget the tennis balls and nighties. *Deliver This!* moms tell the most useful—and most useless—items to pack for the hospital:

• PUT IN THE BAG: Camera, list of phone numbers, iPod, lip balm, socks, bottles of water, cookies to share with the nurses and your visitors, crappy yet enjoyable magazines, your own pillow, travel Scrabble, blank birth announcements.

• LEAVE AT HOME: Books, thong underwear, any new clothes (especially fancy pajamas or robes), candles, incense, lavender oil.

• BONUS TIP: Make your husband or partner physically pack the bag so he knows what's in there and where it is. "When I was in labor, I was dying for ChapStick, and I wound up screaming between contractions, 'No! In the side pocket! On the outside!'" said one mom.

---

perfectly happy to stay put. And then, just after 7:00 PM, I easily gave birth to a healthy little girl, without having to suffer through any more agonizing pain. And no one can tell me that my daughter—who builds elaborate Lego contraptions, can quote *Wallace & Gromit* at length, and makes us all laugh with her ridiculously silly "tushy dance"—is any less amazing for having been born that way.

Somewhere between 50 and 60 percent of women who give birth in a hospital wind up asking for an epidural (in larger hospitals where there is an anesthesiologist on call 24/7, the numbers can be much higher).[1] They do it for pretty much the same reasons I did. Labor can be unbearably painful, and there comes a point when mothers-to-be say, *"Alright, enough already!"* No matter what they may have planned for their childbirth experience, the pain becomes the single most defining element—and they want nothing more at that moment than to make it go away and turn the experience into something more positive.

Most of the women I spoke with adamantly argued that they would rather experience the delivery of their child as a relaxed, serene new mom than as a stressed-out, exhausted one. They didn't want the first sounds their baby would hear to be screams of anguish. They wanted to actually *enjoy* the delivery, and they felt that was impossible in their pre-epidural state of mind. The idea that women have valiantly borne the pain of childbirth throughout the millennia before the advent of anesthetics is of absolutely no comfort. They just say, "Well, it's a good thing I'm giving birth now and not then!" There is a definite feeling of, *We have the technology, people! Why not take advantage of it?!*

The theme of so many of these birth stories was much the same—how the epidural divided labor into two entirely different experiences. "When I went into labor, I was Strep B-positive, so I couldn't have the epidural until they got the antibiotics going," said Alice, an engineer and mother of two in Boulder, Colorado. "It took forever—I was sitting up on my knees, cursing, and my mind was on nothing but the pain. I got the epidural when I was at six centimeters, and I was so glad when it kicked in! It was such a huge relief. My sister had a natural birth, and I think that was great for her, but it's not for me. She runs marathons, too, and I don't really get the point of that either. I just didn't see anything positive in the pain."

And yes, there are natural-birth moms who swear they were able to reach a Zenlike state through safer means than drugs, but to really be able to control the pain naturally, you have to have a specific belief system, a highly developed mind-body connection, and most significantly, a desire for this kind of birth that is so powerful that you are able to push through the difficult part of the labor without giving in to the easier and virtually guaranteed results of an epidural.

There is an ardent skepticism among epidural-loving moms that natural pain relief can work at all (and as any natural-birth educator will tell you, if you don't believe in it, it's *not* going to work). So instead of taking that leap of faith in our bodies, we take a leap of faith in modern medical science.

While putting an immediate end to the agony is the number-one reason women state for getting an epidural (hell, it's numbers two through ten as well), there is a long list of perks that come with the dissipation of pain. First of all, there's the rest factor: Bracing yourself for contractions every couple of minutes is exhausting work, and you may be doing that for five, ten, even twenty hours, especially with your first baby. The ability to let go and relax for a little while is a beautiful thing, and it's just what many moms feel they need to recharge themselves for the pushing portion of the evening (of all the things I've heard natural-birth moms claim, none have said they were able to sleep while in heavy labor).

"I thought I would be one of those superwomen who could just shoot a baby out with no drugs, but my labor took much longer than I ever expected," says Jennie, an actress and mother of two in Los Angeles. "After I had been in and out of the hospital, and then was having intense contractions for nine hours with only a short break in between each one, my doctor said, 'You're exhausted, you need to sleep,' and I said, 'You know what? I really do!' So I asked for the epidural, and I have absolutely no regrets about it."

I've heard a lot of dads joke that *they* could use some pain relief to get through their partner's labor, and while I doubt they would go so far as to roll up their shirt, lean over, and ask for a hit of that epidural themselves, they do get a sort of "secondhand high" from the mom's pain relief, as my husband will gladly tell you. As soon as I relaxed, so did Jeremy. And even though I was the one going through the physical act of childbirth, I had to remember that this was a huge, life-altering moment for *him* as well, one he should be able to enjoy with me.

I was impressed by the stories natural-birth moms told me about their partners supporting them through labor, rubbing their backs and massaging their legs. I wish I could have experienced that kind of team spirit, but it just wasn't going to happen. For me and so many other women I spoke with, the only possible reaction to the hardest part of unmedicated labor is to push everyone else away. This adds an extra layer of torture for men, in particular, who love to fix things, and can only stand by and watch as the person they love suffers in pain, while they simmer in the knowledge that there is nothing they can do to make it better. "When my contractions hit, I was doubled over, and it was just terrible for my husband to watch me like that," said Elaine, a web publisher and mother of two in New York. "Every time he tried to ask me something or talk to me, I was extremely short with him. After I had the epidural, it was a much more enjoyable experience for both of us."

Not only does the pain relief help you interact with your partner again, it also allows you to listen to all those other people who are trying to help you have a safe and effective labor. When it is time to do the hard work of pushing the baby out—or even more crucially, to make informed decisions about your labor—it can be much easier to focus when you are in a calm, lucid state. In fact, I have spoken to women who believe that they were only able to *avoid* a C-section because they had the epidural. "My baby was in a weird position, with his arm over his head, so my labor stalled," Alice told me. "The doctor had me roll to one side and try all kinds of positions, which I'm sure I would not have been able to do if I was in immense pain. I was finally able to deliver him vaginally. Who knows, if I had not had the epidural, I might not have had the energy and focus to try those positions, and then I might have wound up with a C-section."

Moms who wind up asking for an epidural are by no means universal in their feelings about them. There are many women who tell their doctors from day one that they want to get an epidural as soon as humanly possible. (While many doctors, including mine, insist on waiting until you are at least four centimeters dilated before allowing an epidural, there is a growing trend to provide pain relief as soon as it is requested; recent studies in both the *New England Journal of Medicine* and the *American Journal of Obstetrics & Gynecology* have shown that early epidurals are no more likely

*"I never thought my little brother would be there, but he was right beside my head, promising me a double scoop of Rocky Road if I pushed harder. When the doctor asked my husband to cut the cord, he said no, and then my mom said no, so I said, 'Give me the damn scissors,' and I cut it myself!"*

to result in a C-section than late ones and may in fact speed labor along.)[2,3]

But there seem to be just as many moms who prefer to play the "wait and see" game. They figure they'll labor naturally as long as possible, and then ask for an epidural when the pain gets to be too much. Interestingly, this attitude appears to be relegated only to first-time births; by the time the second baby comes around, there's an attitude of, *Okay, been there, done that. I've experienced the pain of childbirth and I don't see the need to do it again.* "With my first baby, I tried to be tough and hold off on the epidural as long as possible," recalled Regina, a stay-at-home mother of two in Pasadena, Maryland. "My contractions started on a Sunday, and I didn't deliver until Tuesday. When I finally went to the hospital, I was exhausted, but I was still only at three centimeters. I thought, *There is no way I can do this anymore,* and I asked for the epidural. When I had my second baby three years later, I was much more relaxed because my expectations were that I would get the drugs when I needed them. So instead of feeling defeated when I got the medication, I just felt smart."

I know, I can see you out there: All the natural-birth advocates who are reading this are shaking their heads and saying, *But what about the baby?*

And the medicated-birth moms' response: *Give me a break.*

In fact, most mainstream, medicated-birth moms are

fairly stunned when it is suggested that they are taking a risk by having a baby in a hospital with drugs. First of all, they find it illogical that natural-birth advocates would applaud a woman who would intentionally have a baby at home, far away from the safety net of a hospital, yet would question the motives of a woman who opts to deliver in a hospital where blood transfusions, respirators, and skilled surgeons are right there—just in case you should need them. Whatever real or imaginary risks there might be from extra germs in a hospital atmosphere are so vastly outweighed by the concrete benefits of delivering there that it's not even open for discussion.

Now, I'm not much of a gambler, but I see this as two different ways of playing the same odds: Moms who deliver *outside* a hospital say that 90 percent of all deliveries are normal, healthy, uncomplicated—you can do it by yourself with a bathtub, a pair of scissors, and a warm towel. Mainstream moms look at those odds and say, *I hear you, but doesn't that mean that one in ten women will run into problems?* That's a pretty significant slice of the pie. One in ten means that at least a dozen or so women I know will have a baby who comes early, stops breathing, or has the umbilical cord around his neck. One in ten means that somewhere in my extended family there will be a woman whose blood pressure spikes, who hemorrhages after delivery, or develops a blood-clotting disorder. *What if that person turns out to be me?* "Delivering in a hospital is like wearing a seat belt," explained Karen, a mother of three in Ames, Iowa.

"Chances are you will get in your car and go for a drive and get to where you need to go with no problems. But you put on your seat belt anyway."

Now, about that epidural, that blessed, lovely, wonderful invention that—for women who want it—has the magical ability to turn our experience of childbirth inside out, to convert it from a gritty, dark melodrama into a delightful, Technicolor musical. Do the women who choose to have an epidural worry that they are risking the health and welfare of their baby for a few hours of pain relief?

No, they don't. Most of the women I interviewed had never (or only vaguely) heard about the theory of cascading intervention, and when I explained it to them, they suspected it was just another way to make women feel guilty about their choices. They filed it in the same category with vaccination alarmists and radical veganism.

In a way, there is a bit of willful blindness involved. The benefit of an epidural is so great, so overwhelmingly positive, that very few women who are predisposed to ask for one are going to snoop around the natural-birth literature, looking for a reason to change their mind. But what we do know is this: The drugs have been tested and approved, and they have been widely used for decades. If your doctor, who has attended hundreds of births before, says it's okay, then that is more than enough reason for most of us to say "yes."

And even though I put absolutely no thought into this *before* I had a baby, I have researched it since then, and the interesting thing is that most of the studies that natural-birth advocates point to as proof that epidurals slow down labor making delivery more difficult and leading to an increased risk of C-sections, forceps delivery, and vacuum delivery are based on older epidurals with far higher doses of narcotics than the diluted solutions that are commonly used now. They also do not take into account the fact that women who have difficult labors with large babies in awkward positions—the kinds of pregnancies that are most likely to lead to a C-section anyway—are going to have longer, more painful labors, making them more likely to ask for an epidural in the first place.

I was fascinated by the results of a 2001 study by the National Institute of Child Health and Human Development, which found, after analyzing more than 1,000 hospital records, that epidurals did *not* increase the rate of C-sections, and did not increase the rate of births requiring forceps or vacuum extraction. The only measurable difference was that women who had an epidural added an average of twenty-five minutes to their time in labor.[4]

Twenty-five minutes.

That's not even the length of one rerun of *The Odd Couple*. That's less time than it takes to brew a cup of coffee and read one feature article in the *New Yorker*. Ask any medicated-birth mom if she would be willing to tack on an extra twenty-five minutes to her labor if it means not suffering in pain, and she will say, *Hell, yeah!* Besides, it's all relative: Twenty-five minutes of easy, medicated labor go by at roughly the same pace as twelve seconds of hard labor.

But let's, for the moment, forget about that study and the dozens of others by respected researchers at top institutions that shed major doubt on the supposed epidural-C-section connection. Let's say we conceded that the epidural *could* increase your chances of having a C-section by 10 percent or so. When I ran that possibility by the medicated-birth moms I interviewed, only a couple said that such a statistic would make them think twice about getting drugs. The rest mulled it over and agreed with Wendy, a stay-at-home mother of two in Pensacola, Florida, who said, "You know what? I would still have the epidural, because the reward outweighs that risk by such a huge margin." While surgical birth is often seen by natural-birth moms as the great big scary bogey-man, for medicated-birth moms it is more like that annoying neighbor who lives down the block. The whole premise of the "cascade of interventions" that natural-moms so ardently wish to avoid is that it inevitably leads to a C-section, which is seen as unnatural, dangerous, and traumatic, compromising the initial bonding between mother and child.

Now, while a surgical birth would not be the *first* choice of any of the women I interviewed for this chapter, it is not seen as a horrendous, unthinkable failure. Everyone knows someone who had a C-section, most for medical reasons but some simply because they preferred the procedure (see Chapter 10). And while C-sections are generally viewed as disappointing and painful for the mother, they are also given their props as a miraculous procedure that can save a baby who otherwise would have died. If an epidural *were* to inevitably lead to a C-section, said Teresa, a mother of three in Sparta, New Jersey, she would be at peace with that: "I understand it's difficult to recover from a C-section, but however bad it might be, it could not possibly compare with the torture of spending fourteen hours feeling like a bear was trying to rip me apart from the inside out."

Just as the theoretical possibility of an increased risk of C-section didn't set off many alarms for those in the epidural fan club, neither did the idea of the drugs crossing the placenta and reaching the baby. Many of these women said they asked their doctors or childbirth instructors about it, and they were assured that it was a tiny dose and there was no evidence that it had any adverse effect on babies. And considering that most of these moms would be stocking up on the infant Motrin and taking the baby for vaccinations soon anyway, a tiny drop of pain reliever was hardly seen as a catastrophe.

We do know that there are plenty of possible side effects you may experience if you get an epidural: Numbness, itching, and nausea are common, and 1 or 2 percent of moms will suffer through a nasty postpartum headache.[5] There is the chance the mother's blood pressure will drop, and if she is on the epidural for more than six hours, there's a chance that she will develop a slight fever. (Neither of these side effects is life-threatening, and both can be treated immediately if necessary.) We read about these risks in pregnancy books, get handouts about them in childbirth classes, and then, *just in case we forget,* we are required to sign a release form spelling out all the gory details in that last excruciating moment before the anesthesiologist will do his thing.

But all these side effects are viewed as risks to the *mother's* health, not the baby's (though if you do get a fever, the baby might be treated with antibiotics, and if you get a screaming headache, you might not be so keen on nursing). And since we are all consenting adults, we can make that decision for ourselves. For many medicated-birth moms, it's another version of "Get your politics off my body."

Whereas natural-birth moms tend to roll off a reading list of books and articles promoting natural birth, medicated-birth moms tend to stick with the mainstream stuff—*What to Expect When You're Expecting, The Girlfriends' Guide to Pregnancy,* magazines like *Fit Pregnancy* and *Parenting*—which do not purport to have an agenda (though of course some might argue that they have an agenda just by being mainstream). There is a new crop of books that are more upfront about promoting a medicated method of birth, such

## Can Sex Jumpstart Your Labor?

*Deliver This!* moms tried many interesting methods for naturally inducing their labor—drinking herbal tea, eating spicy food, walking up and down the stairs—but the most common tactic was having lots of sex. All that nookie may have helped pass the time, but it probably didn't do much for labor: A 2006 report in *Obstetrics & Gynecology* found that women who had sex in the final weeks of pregnancy delivered on average at 39.9 weeks; those who abstained delivered at 39.3 weeks.[6]

as *Enjoy Your Labor,* by Gilbert Grant, and *Easy Labor: Every Woman's Guide to Choosing Less Pain and More Joy During Childbirth,* by William Camann and Kathryn Alexander, but those have not yet reached the cultlike devotion of natural-birth classics such as *Ina May's Guide to Childbirth,* by Ina May Gaskin, or *Birthing from Within: An Extra-Ordinary Guide to Childbirth Preparation,* by Pam England and Rob Horowitz.

Instead, mainstream moms tend to base their decisions on their own observations, a sort of "show me the money" school of thought: They look around at all the women they know who have given birth in hospitals, who have had epidurals to ease their pain, who have had interventions deemed medically necessary by their doctors, and they see that those women walked out of the hospital with a healthy baby who was just as adorable as any child born at the most holistic birth center. They look at their friends' children and they cannot see any difference in temperament, personality, or achievement in those who were born naturally and those who got a little taste of medication on their way out of the womb. "You know, I have plenty of friends who delivered naturally who have sucky relationships with their kids!" said Leah, a lawyer and mother of three in Salem, Oregon. "Your birth experience does not necessarily translate into life, and whether you go natural or have drugs or have a C-section, it does not diminish in any way how you feel about your child."

From my vantage point, having spoken to so many

mothers who have given birth in so many different ways, I can truly say that I see no difference in which children have closer relationships with their parents, which kids get into gifted programs at school, which kids write the sweetest sayings on their Valentine's Day cards, and which are the most serene. I know of children born in the gentlest, most idyllic settings who grew up to be whiny and difficult. I know of children born in emergency C-sections who grew up to be delightfully sweet-natured. It just doesn't seem to matter.

"I think the only connection between the type of birth and the kind of kid you get is in the mother's mind, and if you buy into the idea that there's a connection, everything you see is going to feed into it," says Randi, a teacher and mother of one in Brooklyn, New York. "If you read that epidurals cause attention-deficit issues, of course every time your kid doesn't listen to you, you'll say, 'Oh, it must have been the epidural!' I just did not pay any attention to any of that. And except when my son wakes me up at 5:30 AM, he's a pretty great kid."

One major irony I found in this whole debate is that while some natural-birth moms are quick to blame the media and society for promoting a unwarranted fear of childbirth pain, several of those very same moms admitted being terrified of the epidural needle, which, for me, was as gentle as being tickled with a Q-Tip, compared with the full-body viper grip of a contraction. When you hear certain women describe the injection—*A giant needle is jabbed in your spine, and if you move during the injection, you can be paralyzed!*—well, sure, it's kind of scary. But I found that in reality, it was far easier than getting blood taken. First and foremost, you can't possibly watch the needle go in, and frankly, if you're experiencing enough labor pain to request an epidural, the sharp little prick of a needle is a pretty nice distraction.

If knowledge conquers fear, let's get the battle started by getting down some facts: An *epidural* is an injection of painkilling medication into the space between the vertebrae and the spinal fluid. After your back is cleansed and a local anesthetic is injected (that's the pinch you feel), a needle is inserted, and a catheter about the width of a pencil lead is threaded through the needle; the needle is removed and the catheter is taped in place. The epidural takes about fifteen minutes to kick in, and the steady flow of medication through the catheter lasts as long as you need it. In most instances, the dosage will be turned down while you push, and at a few hospitals, doctors may even leave the catheter in for twenty-four hours *after* labor if you wish to continue a low dose of the anesthetic while you recover. With a *spinal*, the medication is injected directly into your spinal fluid. There is no catheter—it's just one dose that kicks in almost immediately but only lasts for a couple of hours. A spinal tends to be used when a woman asks for pain relief when she is very close to delivering.

The newest generation of "walking" epidurals are actually a combination of a spinal and an epidural. They give a much lower dose of medication (as little as one-tenth the amount that was used in earlier epidurals),[7] leaving the abdomen numb while allowing the patient to retain feeling in the lower half of her body. "After I had the epidural, I was allowed to sit on the birthing ball as long as my mother or husband was nearby," Randi told me. "Before I had the epidural, the ball was no help—I was desperately moving around, trying to find a comfortable position, until I realized there was no such thing! Once the anesthesiologist showed up and gave me the drugs, I was bouncing on the ball and I was really up for the labor, ready to be a part of it instead of just saying, 'Knock me out and wake me when the baby's out.' "

Unlike Randi, however, most women don't do any walking with a walking epidural, since they need to be hooked up to an IV and probably have a continuous fetal monitor strapped to their abdomens. And really, by that point you are just happy to kick back and relax. But the lower dose of the combined spinal-epidural means two important things: One, there is an even tinier amount of medication making its way to the baby; and two, the mother can have much more control over the active (pushing) phase of labor. I can testify that I felt *every* push during both of my deliveries—I distinctly remember that "ring of fire" when the baby's head pushed through. I doubt that my active phase of labor was at all slowed down by the epidural: My first daughter, Bellamy, came out in less than thirty minutes, and my second, Molly, in less than five. On the other hand, I have talked to moms who had *no* drugs, yet wound up pushing for hours.

I have not found any evidence that epidurals make you

groggy, a common concern I heard from natural-birth moms. Narcotics like Stadol and Demerol can make you loopy, and they have the potential to make your baby sleepy, too, since they are delivered in higher doses and go to work on your entire body, including your brain.[8] But since the epidural is concentrated only on the section that needs relief—your abdomen—it does not have the same effect. In fact, pretty much all the moms I spoke with reported being more alert, more involved, and more "present" for the birth after having the epidural.

It's pretty difficult for women who choose an epidural to think about anything other than the pain factor when contemplating the idea of natural birth, but there are plenty of other points where the two sides diverge. All but a handful of the natural-birth moms I spoke to were adamantly opposed to *any* kind of intervention, including induction, augmentation (using Pitocin to push along a meandering labor), episiotomy, and internal fetal monitoring, things that medicated-birth moms often accept as necessary parts of the whole hospital-epidural package.

While some of those interventions are being phased out in American hospitals (episiotomy has decreased from 70 percent of all vaginal births in the early '80s to around 20 percent in 2002),[9] the artificial induction of labor has rapidly increased. In 1989, only around 8 percent of births were induced; today it is around 20 percent.[10,11] A Pitocin pump is the method you hear about most often, but your doctor can also get things moving by breaking your water, stripping your membranes (the doctor manually separates your placenta from your uterus), or inserting a prostaglandin medication into your vagina.

Women get their labor started for all kinds of reasons. For all those women waddling around a week or two after their due date, freaking out about the possibility of giving birth to a twelve-pound baby with a head the size of a honeydew, inductions are often a welcome end to the waiting game. Other women are induced because signs of preeclampsia or diabetes in the mother or distress in the child convince the doctor that the risks of leaving the baby in are greater than the risks of getting him out.

But if you listen to the chatter on message boards or talk to moms who may already be suspicious of the medical establishment, you will hear plenty of theories that the rate of inductions is skyrocketing simply because doctors—and sometimes mothers—are looking for the convenient way out. They are looking for a way to bend the unpredictable timing of childbirth around their own personal schedules so as to not ruin their weekend plans or be woken at 3:00 AM. Some women would have you believe there is an epidemic of doctors all over the country scrolling through their PDAs and saying, "Oh, damn, I've got tickets to the basketball game on Saturday. Let's go in and get that baby out on Thursday, shall we?"

And I have to say, there is a bit of truth to this. In my research I have come across some pretty lame reasons for inducing labor: One woman told me that she jokingly scolded her favorite nurse for planning a vacation during her due date; her doctor overheard her, and the next thing she knew, she had a date to induce before her nurse boarded the plane. The National Center for Health Statistics confirms that babies are much less likely to be born on the weekend than during the workweek: In 2002, the average number of babies born on a Tuesday was two-thirds higher than those born on a Sunday, and though scheduled C-sections have much to do with this, there was also a notable difference in the number of vaginal births.[12]

Artificial induction has its own risks—many women reported that their contractions were harder and closer together after they got the Pitocin; some women who had hoped to avoid an epidural found that the induction quashed any hope of using natural pain control; and there is the concern that if the induction is scheduled before the due date, the baby's lungs might not have matured enough to work on their own. (Due dates and estimated baby weights are a notoriously fallible guessing game.) "I had to let go of the idea that it was going to be exciting and dramatic, and just accept that it was so artificial," said Jennie, who was induced because she was showing no signs of starting labor and her doctor worried that if she went too far past her due date, she wouldn't be able to push a post-term baby out of her four-foot, ten-inch frame. Still, despite the letdown, she was glad she was able to deliver her son vaginally.

Despite the risks and the clinical aspect of their birth stories, I met moms who were absolutely thrilled with their inductions. "When I was due with my third child, we had just moved out to the boondocks, and the nearest hospital was a half hour away," said Teresa. "When I went four days past my due date, the doctor suggested we schedule an induction, since he was worried that my labor would go too quickly for me to get to the hospital. I was a little wary, but then I realized it would be so much easier to know when it was happening so I could prepare the kids and call the baby sitter. I drove myself to the hospital, where they gave me Pitocin and broke my water. I thought it would be more painful than my previous births, but it wasn't at all. I got the epidural right away. Then, an hour later, I felt some cramping, so I called the doctor in and asked if I needed to turn up the epidural. He was like, 'No, you're ready to push!' It was so quick, my husband almost didn't get there in time. I did half a push and then one more push, and the baby was out. I could not believe how easy, painless, and uncomplicated it was. It almost made me consider having a fourth child."

In a way, mainstream medicated-birth moms think about hospitals the same way they think about airports: An airport is big and noisy, the food usually sucks, stressed-out people are scurrying about, the air-conditioning is either busted or turned up way too high—but that's where the airplanes are, and if you want to get to that tropical island with the conch fritters and fruity drinks, you gotta buy that ticket. And if you want to have a safe, pain-free birth, you go to a hospital. Medicated-birth moms are more than happy to tell you all the reasons they *didn't* like their hospital experience: I heard complaints about sharing a tiny room with a stranger, being woken by PA announcements every half hour, having a doctor who doesn't show up until the baby is practically pulling himself out, or getting the newbie anesthesiologist who has to try three times before getting the needle in the right spot.

Despite it all, those were seen as minor inconveniences—the price we pay to give birth in a place where all your health needs will be taken care of, where a team of highly skilled professionals are available around the clock in case something unexpected comes up. "I've worked in a neonatal intensive care unit, and I have seen a lot of things that can go wrong," said Holly, a nurse and mother of two in Goldsboro, North Carolina. "I know that had they been born in a place where medical care was not right there and ready, the outcome could have been very bad. So many things can happen in the first twenty-four hours after birth, and I want to be somewhere where they can help me."

I found that moms who choose medicated hospital vaginal birth are often pretty rattled by stories they've heard about friends and relatives—or strangers in a magazine—who had traumatic childbirth experiences. I was told about cousins' babies born at home who had alarmingly low Apgar scores (the assessments given at one and five minutes after birth, based on factors such as how well the baby is breathing and how pink his skin tone is), neighbors' babies who had to be revived, sisters' babies born with collapsed lungs. I heard about mothers who started hemorrhaging on the delivery table who would have died if they had been any-where but the hospital. The moms know that these cases are the exception, rather than the rule, but these are these stories that resonate, that play on a constant loop in their minds when they lie awake at night, wondering what it will be like to leap into the great unknown of childbirth.

The main thing medicated-childbirth moms love about hospitals is simply that they are overflowing with doctors. Those same people who are dismissed as arrogant by out-of-hospital moms are seen as dragon-slaying white knights by the rest of us. Just as we always hope to elect a president who is smarter than we are (I did say "hope"), most of us want a doctor who knows more than we do, too. Almost every one of the medicated-birth moms I spoke to mentioned a relative or friend in the medical field—a mother who's a physician or a friend who's a nurse—and they had the utmost respect for their training and knowledge.

"My mother always instilled in me a great respect for doctors," said Paula, a mother of four in Paramus, New Jersey. "Frankly, I would rather have too much doctor involvement in my delivery than too little." Some moms said they considered writing out a birth plan but in the end decided it was a waste of time, since they were more than happy to defer to their doctor on any big medical decisions.

And you know what? I think that's okay. I think trust is a good thing. But I also believe that trust has to be earned.

Which is why you can't count on having a satisfying hospital birth if you choose your doctor by thumbing through your insurance manual and picking the person whose office is closest to your favorite coffee bar. As I have said, with every birth choice, the more work you put into finding a practitioner who fits your philosophies, temperament, and priorities, the easier it will be for you to enjoy your baby's birth with the confidence that he or she is making the best decisions for you. And start early—you don't want to wait until your legs are spread and she's picking up the scissors to ask for her opinion on episiotomies. If you feel you are being rushed through appointments, be aggressive and insist on scheduling a time to discuss your expectations and concerns about things such as induction and pain relief. And if you don't like what your doctor has to say, *find one whose answers you do like.* Even people with the stingiest insurance in the world will likely have more than one option for their OB. Because believe me, if you think your doctor is cold, standoffish, alarmist, or patronizing during your prenatal appointments, it's not going to miraculously get better when you are naked on the table and ready to deliver.

As much as I loved my doctor, it took me a couple of tries before I found her. I had a couple of false starts: My uptown doctor seemed more interested in her fabulous wardrobe than in my questions about birth control; my first downtown doctor had a brusque, no-nonsense manner and wanted to schedule laser surgery because she thought that I might—*might*—have a case of endometriosis that was keeping me from getting pregnant (a month after I switched to a less laser-happy doctor, I was pregnant with no intervention at all). When I met Dr. Masch, I immediately felt comfortable with her. I thought, *Now this is a woman who gets me. This is someone who will listen to me and instinctively know what I would want, even if I can't express it during labor.* And though I really didn't put much thought into how I was going to give birth, by listening to my nesting instinct and choosing this doctor and that hospital, I really was making the decision that was best for me.

"Eyes on the prize, eyes on the prize."

This is a phrase I heard over and over in my research. Natural-birth moms used it to explain how focusing on the end result of all their hard work helped them push through the worst of the pain. Medicated moms sing a different version of that same tune. *Eyes on the prize—don't worry about controlling all the details of labor, since the only thing that matters is coming home with a healthy baby.* If your baby won't budge and you have to be induced, that doesn't matter. If you feel so much pain that you cry out for an epidural, that doesn't matter. Instead of focusing on the *process*, medicated moms focus on the end result. They simply feel that if they can get through the process and win the same prize at the end—a beautiful baby—then why should they have to suffer excruciating pain to get there? "My whole focus was on the outcome," said Holly. "I really didn't care how I got there, I only cared that I came out with a healthy baby. After being pregnant for all those months, I was really just anxious to start my life as a new mom, so that's what I focused on."

And that's what this whole crazy debate comes down to: We are *all* becoming moms, and if a mother-to-be will feel more empowered and triumphant and healthy and ready to tackle motherhood after a natural birth, then she should absolutely go forward with a natural birth. But if she feels more secure, more comfortable, more ready to be a parent after a medicated hospital birth, she should proudly and guiltlessly do that and go for the drugs.

The thing that really angers moms who opt for medicated births is the idea that this kind of scenario is somehow second-rate. There are certainly trade-offs—as there are with every single kind of birth experience—

*"We decided not to find out the gender of our baby until it came out, but I was convinced I was having a boy. Everyone told me so, from my family to strangers on the street. So when the doctor said, 'It's a girl!' I yelled, 'No fucking way!' which is apparently not what new mothers usually say."*

but they are so far outweighed by the pleasure of enjoying one's labor instead of struggling through it that women are thrilled to make those trades. Medicated-birth moms reject the idea that their kind of birth can't be as rewarding and beautiful as a natural birth. One of the moms I interviewed had an epidural but still reached down and caught her own baby; others told me they cut the cord themselves. Unless the baby had a health issue that needed immediate attention, everyone who wanted to was able to nurse within the first few minutes after birth. There were cheering siblings, weeping grandparents, beaming cousins with video cameras. Though they may not experience that huge rush of triumph that natural-birth moms describe, there were still plenty of blissed-out moms.

"You know what? After I talked to a lot of other women about their experiences, it became very clear that once the baby is out, it's very difficult to recall the exact details of labor anyway," said Raven, a writer and mother of one in New York. "I was a little disappointed that I needed an epidural and Pitocin, but they really helped my labor speed along with little pain. And the actual birth was wonderful! It was me, my boyfriend, my mom, a doctor, and a nurse in a lovely room overlooking upper Manhattan. My boyfriend and a nurse held my legs up as I pushed, and everyone cheered me on like it was a sporting event. It was truly wonderful."

## CHAPTER EIGHT

# MURPHY BROWN, LABOR INSTRUCTOR: MEDIA *and* CHILD-BIRTH

T he person who taught me the most about childbirth was not my high school health teacher or my doctor. It was Murphy Brown.

That's right, Murphy Brown, the fictional TV reporter played by Candice Bergen, the one who had a philosophy-spouting housepainter named Eldin and who got into a real-life brawl with Dan Quayle over the ethics of single motherhood.

I don't think I'm alone in looking to the media for role models when it comes to labor and delivery. After all, lots of women I know are put off by birth gurus such as Dr. Sears. (I personally have issues with any man telling me how birth "should" feel.) And though Ina May may be popular in certain circles, I had never heard of her. I had plenty of friends who had delivered children in birthing centers, in hospitals, with drugs, without drugs, but I never thought to ask them questions such as, *What does it feel like to push through a contraction?* Or, *Does it really feel like bad menstrual cramps, or is that being way too optimistic?* Or, *How do you make it through the first few hours until you get to have the epidural?*

My husband and I dutifully sat through those childbirth videos in the class we took at the hospital where I delivered, but truthfully, I don't remember a thing about them. I only remember glancing around at my classmates and noticing that the men all squirmed in their chairs and looked at their watches, while the women, hopped up on pregnancy hormones, honked into tissues and dabbed away at tears. I think I mustered up a tear or two, but nothing like the waterworks I produced when Murphy sang "(You Make Me Feel Like) A Natural Woman" to her newborn.

So as a product of the media age—part of the first generation taught to read by *Sesame Street* and one of the first teenagers to listen to pop songs on MTV—it makes sense that I, and many of my peers, learned about childbirth from TV.

Here's a newsflash, pundits of America: The biggest influence on how women view childbirth is not their doctors, their insurance companies, or women's magazines. It's television. More specifically, it's cable television. To be even more specific, it's *A Baby Story,* the childbirth reality show on The Learning Channel. When I asked the women I interviewed where their most vivid images of childbirth came from, *A Baby Story* was listed roughly ten times more than any other source. "I was obsessed with *A Baby Story* when I was pregnant," Randi said. "I watched it five times a week for seven straight months." Shanna told me that her OB gave her explicit instructions to stop watching the show because she became fixated on how much pain the women were in. The moms mention plenty of sitcoms and movies, as well as websites like BabyCenter.com, magazines like *Fit Pregnancy*, and books like *What to Expect* and *The Girlfriends' Guide*, but reality TV beat them all.

**Star Babies**

Celebrity births that *Deliver This!* moms found most fascinating: Britney Spears, Katie Holmes, Gwyneth Paltrow ("I read she was in labor for seventy hours before her doctor 'made her' get an epidural. Give me a break!"), Kate Hudson, Brooke Shields, and Jane Seymour ("How the hell did she look so good after having twins?").

As I tried to gauge which media images of childbirth influenced moms the most, I wasn't just trying to compile a Nielsen-like list of the top ten birth scenes of all time—I was attempting to unravel part of the mystery of what makes certain birth choices right for some women and absolutely wrong for others. I wanted to see how the different images we absorb from the world around us brew in our brains and bring us to our ultimate decisions about where we feel safe and how we feel most empowered about giving birth.

I looked over the emails and transcripts from all my interviews, and a very telling pattern began to emerge. Almost uniformly, the women who were the least influenced by pop culture images of birth were the most firmly committed to natural childbirth. A few of the home-birth and birth-center moms admitted to checking out *A Baby Story* ("They actually showed women doing water births!" one mom told me), one remembered watching Gloria give birth to Joey on *All in the Family*, another mentioned the "I don't know nothin' 'bout birthin' babies" scene from *Gone with the Wind*; but they generally dismissed those and other such depictions as edited, scripted, and therefore unreliable. "TV shows and movies seem to be filled with horror stories about birth," a birth-center mom told me. "I tried to avoid them as much as possible."

Now, you could argue here about the chicken and the egg: Does pop culture influence our childbirth choice, or do women who are predisposed to natural birth watch less TV and see fewer movies in the first place? On the one hand, your stereotypical holistic, nature-loving, yoga-practicing, marathon-running natural-birth mom is probably not sitting around her living room watching six hours of TV a night, and she probably doesn't come from a family that watched *I Love Lucy* reruns at the dinner table (and if she did, she probably rejected that habit as firmly as she dismissed fat-laden TV dinners and the five o'clock martini).

But also, by avoiding all the shows that depict childbirth as a dramatic situation filled with all kinds of wacky complications (Gloria Stivic getting stuck in a telephone booth while in labor, for example), these moms are able to reinforce their mind-set that childbirth is a natural, healthy, normal event. One of the most interesting insights on this topic was from a midwife I interviewed who had assisted the births of numerous Mennonite women in her Pennsylvania practice. These "plain community" women had never had any exposure to pop culture births, and therefore they labored differently—they saw childbirth as a regular life event, and seemed to have a lot less fear about it, she told me.

Instead of fictionalized versions of childbirth, natural-birth moms, in general, were way more influenced by real-life testimonials of inspiring births, and by the plethora of books by natural-birth gurus such as Pam England and Henci Goer, and by feminist authors such as Naomi Wolf, whose 2001 book *Misconceptions* detailed her own traumatic emergency C-section.

But most of all, they were influenced by other women. Almost every natural-birth mom could trace her first spark of interest in a nonmedicalized birth back to a friend, a cousin, a teacher, a friend's mom, or a boss who had gone through the process herself and became a de facto childbirth mentor, spreading the gospel of a "better" kind of birth. For some women, the road to natural childbirth began in college, when a women's studies class or a particularly influential professor changed the way they thought about their body—one even mentioned a specific filmstrip she was shown about women in indigenous South American cultures giving birth.

Interestingly, I found that once they were on the path toward natural birth, most of these moms began to reject any book, magazine article, or TV show that might suggest there was another legitimate way to give birth. "I found all of these discussions to be the voice of 'the man' or the largely ignorant woman or doctor," said a mom who had one home birth and one birth-center birth. On the positive side, this tunnel vision helped them stay focused on their plan, and reading only pro-natural materials helped get them in the mental place where you have to be to make it through the physically and mentally challenging job of unmedicated childbirth. But also, by rejecting other points of view, some moms became so entrenched in the "medicine is bad" school of thought that when their birth didn't go as planned, they felt that they had failed (more on this in Chapter 11).

And then there are those who tuned in to *Murphy Brown.*

In May 1992, when I was years away from even entertaining the thought of having a child of my own, Murphy gave birth to her baby son on TV. I had seen other TV births, but for some reason, this one burrowed deep into my brain and made a home there. Nine years later, when I was pregnant for the first time and trying to imagine how my birth story would play out, I couldn't help but think of Murphy.

And I have to say, *Murphy Brown* may have been fiction, but it was clearly written by a woman, and for a twenty-two-minute sitcom episode, it painted a fairly accurate picture of giving birth in a hospital. The most vivid image for me was of Murphy shuffling down the hospital corridor in slippers and a hospital gown, pale and sweaty with her TV-star hair hanging in her face, begging her friends,

"Cut me open and get this kid out of me! Use a melonballer if you have to!" Nine years later, there I was, shuffling down a hospital corridor in slippers and a hospital gown, pale and sweaty, growling at my husband and saying, "How long until I can get the epidural?" (Unfortunately, I did not have a team of Emmy-winning writers feeding me clever one-liners to spit out through the pain.)

When I watched this episode again recently, I discovered that many of the other details rang incredibly true to life, not just from my own birth story, but from all the others I have listened to since then: Murphy borrowing a jacket to wear around her soaking pants after her water breaks at work. Murphy being so exhausted after hours of labor that she doesn't want to push. Murphy saying in the middle of a contraction, "I feel like I'm being sucked inside out. Don't be surprised if you see my liver pop out!"

But hidden among the punch lines, there was one scene that stunned me into silence: After Murphy, in excruciating pain, asks her nurse for drugs, the nurse says, "Why don't you wait a half hour? Many moms find they don't need them after all." Then she starts laughing demonically and walks away.

And that's it. There is no more discussion of drugs.

What was up with that? Why would a hospital deny painkilling medicine to someone who so clearly wants and needs it? And more important, why would someone as powerful, aggressive, and loud as Murphy Brown put up with that? *What the hell?*

I rewound—did they give her the epidural and I missed it? Nope. And then, as I watched a dozen more sitcom episodes about childbirth (including *All in the Family, Family Ties, Sex and the City,* and *Friends*), I realized that I couldn't find any mention of any kind of pain relief anywhere. Nada. Except for a few joking references to Lamaze and some comical huffing and puffing, there was nothing being done to relieve these women of their pain. There were no epidurals, no Stadol "to take the edge off," no hot baths, no relaxation tapes, no doulas.

And then it hit me: Pain is a lot funnier than comfort. Watching sweet, pretty Rachel turn into a shrew and growl to Ross, "It feels like I'm trying to blow a Saint Bernard out my ass!" makes much better TV than, say, watching her quietly flip through a copy of *People* while Ross eats a tuna sandwich. In the same way, watching someone breathe while a doula gently massages her lower back is about as entertaining as watching your fingernails grow, so you don't see many women practicing natural pain-relief methods on TV either. What we learn is that childbirth is horribly painful (though not so painful that you can't talk), and there's not much you can do about it except crack jokes.

And it's not only pain relief that drops out of the picture when a sitcom mom gives birth—there is no such thing as Pitocin, there is no such thing as a C-section, there is no such thing as an episiotomy or tear. No matter what complications there are, all it takes is a little pep talk from Dad, an extra push from Mom, and everything turns out peachy keen. After all, on *Friends,* Rachel had a breech baby, Phoebe had triplets, and the woman who gave birth to Monica and Chandler's adopted babies had twins, but the possibility of a cesarean was never mentioned during any of these births.

I have to say that despite the fantastical circumstances of all of these births, some of the details were right on the money. Rachel's fictional delivery room looked exactly like my real one (though when she is switched to the maternity ward, it looks as spacious as a suite at the Four Seasons), and Jennifer Aniston got herself into a very realistic—and realistically unflattering—birth position, knees brushing her ears. If you want to see a very real depiction of the awkwardness of early breastfeeding, watch Miranda on *Sex and the City.* If you want to watch a bravura performance of the grunting and pushing that goes on in active labor by an actress who has clearly been there herself, watch Brenda on *Six Feet Under.*

What's not so real: In the end, after two or three pushes, each mom pops out a baby (or three) who is pink and clean and adorable, and she instantly feels an overwhelming sense of love for it and sings or whispers loving words to it as the credits roll.

Even though these aforementioned births take place in a sitcom fantasy world, at least they acknowledge the fact that a baby comes out of a woman's vagina. If your knowledge of childbirth came from the classic sitcoms from the '50s and '60s that run in the middle of the night on TV Land, you might believe that babies somehow roll out of a suitcase or pop out of the top of a bouffant hairdo. The mother enters the hospital and then, after a commercial break, a nurse holds up a tiny infant. The fathers in these shows don't even get to witness labor, so why should the viewer? (In *I Love Lucy,* the characters weren't even allowed to utter the word "pregnant." Lucy's condition was referred to as "the blessed event.")

The message that sitcoms such as *Lucy* and *The Dick Van Dyke Show* sent was rather appropriate for the "mother as domestic goddess" image that these post-WWII, pre-Vietnam creations espoused. Impending childbirth brings a preternatural sense of serenity and wisdom to the mother, these shows explain, while it turns the father into a raving lunatic who must be cared for by the mom-to-be. Think about it: The reason we love Lucy is that she is crazy, impulsive, and headstrong, but watch her calmly knitting a baby sweater, glowing with a maternal aura of control and sweetness, while Ricky, Ethel, and Fred run about the apartment in mass hysteria, knocking each other over and spilling the contents of the hospital bag. On *Dick Van Dyke,* when Laura goes into labor, she remains her adorable, perfectly coiffed self, while Rob loses his pants and gets a black eye. How could anyone possibly live up to this image of the perfect, nurturing angel who doesn't wince, doesn't grunt, doesn't feel any pain, doesn't make demands, and walks calmly into the hospital while her hysterical husband is brought in by wheelchair?

No wonder everyone in those days just wanted to be knocked out.

Alternative births are almost unheard of on scripted TV. The closest I found to one was the episode of *Family Ties* in which the writers introduced the fourth Keaton child, Andy (Jennifer was going through puberty at that point, so I guess they needed a new paragon of adorableness). Because of one of those only-on-TV complications, earth mother Elyse goes into labor while singing a folk song on a public-TV telethon; hippie dad Steven gets stuck in a snowstorm trying to bring the doctor to his laboring wife. As they wait at the TV station, Young Republican Alex says to his mom, "How can you be so calm? You are about to have a baby in a nonmedical, nonprofessional, nonprofit envi-

### Childbirth + Racism = Classic TV Humor?

In *I Love Lucy,* while Ricky is waiting in the hospital for Lucy to give birth, he changes into his "voodoo" costume for his nightclub act—including an Afro wig and "native" makeup—and winds up scaring all the ladies in the hospital. Twenty years later, as Gloria gives birth on *All in the Family,* Archie shows up at the hospital in costume for his lodge's minstrel show—including an Afro wig and blackface—and scares an old lady in the hospital. Is Archie's costume an homage to Ricky's, or is this just proof that childbirth makes *writers* lose their minds, too?

ronment!" Elyse calmly responds, "Well, honey, I'm in a familiar setting, surrounded by family." Is that a nod to home birthing I heard? Almost.

But still, they cheat on the ending: Minutes before baby Andy comes flying out, the kindly doctor comes flying in to deliver him. Wouldn't it have been more realistic and more interesting to see Elyse squat down in the restroom while

Jennifer pulled out the baby and cut the cord? Ah, well, maybe in the next reunion special.

And wait, let's not forget *ER* and all its medical-drama kin. Back in the '90s, when *ER* was still the hot show that everyone discussed the next day in the office, my pregnant coworker Laura told me she had to stop watching it because it seemed like every week there was another stillborn, preemie, or dying child. If the baby lived, the mother died. When both baby and mother beat the odds and survived till the closing credits, it was only because a handsome, heroic doctor rushed in to save the day. Anyway, we may laugh at Phoebe, we may remember Laura Petrie, we may aspire to be like Elyse Keaton, but in the end we know that these moms and these labors are not truly representative of the real thing. We know they are hyped-up, overly dramatized, and musically scored to get us laughing or crying. We know that actual births by real women would not be deemed remotely interesting enough for television. Right? So how do we explain *A Baby Story*?

Each episode of this half-hour reality show follows one couple as they prepare for their child's birth—and then it shows the birth itself, with only the most sensitive body parts pixelated for modesty. I came late to the *Baby Story* cult, but through the miracle of digital recording, I was able to catch up by watching six or seven episodes in a row for a couple of weeks. And if this had been my only peek into how babies are born, this is what I would have learned: Everyone who gives birth in America is happily married, with a supportive partner and a loving family. They are all clean-cut suburbanites named Susan, Jen, Lisa, Dave, Tom, and Dan. They all have devoted doctors and midwives who listen carefully to all their concerns and guide them expertly through the process. There is a constant loop of cheesy soft jazz playing behind them. And however they choose to give birth, and whatever slight complications there may be on the way, mother and baby always emerge perfectly.

Despite the numbing sameness of the backstories ("We met in college . . . He proposed at our favorite restaurant . . . We always knew we wanted kids . . ."), the series shows a surprising variety of birth choices. I watched a home birth in water, a Hypnobirth, a couple of inducements, and several women who had epidurals (though curiously, while an actual vaginal birth or C-section is not seen as too graphic to show on TV, the injection of an epidural is). I did not detect any editorial discrimination between natural and medicated birth. While these long labors are edited down to a few choice minutes (gotta leave time for those Huggies commercials), they do show the women moaning and dealing with pain in various ways.

I could see how these shows become addictive. Each episode has an incredibly emotional payoff, assuring the viewer that everything will be okay, everything will go according to your plan, your partner will be supportive, your doctor or midwife will perform his or her job impeccably, and the entire delivery room/home/birth center will erupt in a celebration of pure joy. It is a peaceful, optimistic, though somewhat sugarcoated, look at childbirth.

Sugarcoated is about the last word I would use to describe Discovery Health's *Maternity Ward,* another childbirth reality show mentioned by some of the moms. Perhaps this one could be described as arsenic-coated? As a documentary piece of film, this is far more intriguing than *A Baby Story,* but it is *not* a show you want to watch when you are pregnant. Shot in the delivery ward of a hospital for high-risk pregnancies, this is the *ER* of reality shows. Unlike the educated, upper-class women in *A Baby Story,* the patients in *Maternity Ward* were mostly poor, with no insurance and little prenatal care. Many could not speak enough English to communicate with the doctors, and all of them were scared to death.

In one hour, I watched a mother scream in pain and fear as she gave birth fifteen weeks early to a baby in breech position who came out completely blue and had to be revived; I witnessed an emergency C-section performed on a mother who had become unconscious from preeclamptic seizures. There was an emergency transfer from a birth center that ended in a C-section, a newborn who needed heart surgery, a mom who delivered early because of sickle-cell anemia, and a seventeen-year-old who called out for her own mommy as she delivered her premature baby. In *Maternity Ward,* you don't get to hear the birth plans or see the supportive families. In fact, you barely get to hear the mothers' names—the main characters are the fearless interns and attending doctors who do their best to save these tiny, endangered babies.

So whether you are watching *A Baby Story, Maternity*

*Ward, Birth Day Live, Babies: Special Delivery,* or even those videos they show in childbirth classes, you will be seeing a real birth, but it is still carefully chosen, carefully edited, and carefully manipulated to create a sense of drama and play with your emotions.

So what does this all mean? In the end, every media image we have of birth, whether it is an actress cracking one-liners while making funny faces, a homemaker in New Jersey inviting a camera crew into her delivery room, or a photo of an "orgiastic birth" in a book about spiritual midwifery, it has been carefully spun through someone else's agenda. Unless you are actually there, live, at someone's birth, you will always have to guess what the editors, writers, and producers chose to leave out. But as unreliable as these images are, they comprise a good chunk of what makes up our childbirth philosophy. This also means that the great divide between natural-birth moms and medicated-birth moms is made even bigger, since these images from pop culture and literature steer us toward a certain type of birth and then, once we have chosen our team, take us even further away from considering the alternatives. Just as a mom dead-set on getting an epidural is not going to pick up a book about "gentle birth," a mom who is dead-set on home birth is not going to watch a TV show that presents hospital birth as an acceptable, appealing choice.

I have to wonder what my two daughters will think about all this in twenty or thirty years when they are getting ready to have babies of their own. Will there be more choices then, or fewer? Will they watch reruns of *Sex and the City* or *Friends* or *Everybody Loves Raymond* and think their depictions of childbirth are as quaint and obsolete as *I Love Lucy* seems to me? Will there be a new cable network called "C! All C-sections All the Time"? Will they roll their eyes and mutter to themselves when I try to hand them this book? Will they get dragged to a lecture on women's health by their college roommates and change the way they think about their bodies?

I'll keep a tape of *Murphy Brown* around just in case.

## CHAPTER NINE

# OUT *the* EMERGENCY EXIT: PREPLANNED, MEDICALLY ADVISED C-SECTION

*I always knew there was a good chance I would have a C-section, since half of all twin deliveries turn out that way. Around my seventh month, my doctor discovered that the baby who was closest to the exit was in breech position and there was no way to turn her, so I was going to have a C-section for sure. Frankly, that was just fine with me. I remember hearing a comedian who compared childbirth to passing a glazed ham through your nostril. How could that not hurt? I was on modified bed rest for the last three weeks, and they were monitoring me pretty closely. The sonogram at week thirty-six showed that one of the babies was losing amniotic fluid, and it was decided if the next sonogram showed a further decrease, they would perform the C-section that day. When I went in at thirty-seven weeks and one day, my heartburn was so bad I had hardly eaten anything but Popsicles* for a week, and I could barely move. When I told my doctor I hadn't eaten in that long, he decided that between that and the low fluid, it was time to take them out.

It was a breeze, honestly. The worst part for me was the epidural—I was afraid I would flinch and be paralyzed, but of course I didn't. I couldn't feel the surgery at all. My whole body was numb from the chest down. They strapped my arms down on the table like I was on the cross, which was weird, but I guess they don't want you thrashing about. There was a screen up over my chest so I didn't have to watch, and I felt some tugging, but no pain at all. As soon as they took the first baby out, my heartburn immediately vanished—I guess she had been squishing my digestive tract. They lifted her up, all bloody and gloopy, but with her little eyes wide open and looking shocked, like there was a fire drill at her gym while she was changing. Then they took out the second baby, who was a picture-perfect little bundle of screaming baby, just like in the movies.

After that, I had to lie there for about twenty minutes while they put me back together—my husband went to watch the babies being checked out. It didn't feel like a grueling surgical procedure to me. There's such a happy ending, and the mood was as positive as any other birth I've ever heard of, in a pool or with a doula.

**STEPHANIE, EDITOR AND MOTHER OF TWINS**
*New York City*

For most of the past eight chapters, we've been talking about babies who make their grand entrances into this world the traditional way—by sliding down the chute and out the door. The stories may have differed in a million little ways, but the endings were basically the same: ". . . I pushed one last time, and then the baby came out."

But more than one in four babies born in the United States has a very different kind of debut. Instead of getting squeezed down the birth canal by uterine contractions and exiting through the vagina, they get scooped out of the abdomen by the gloved hands of a surgeon. And while some of the women I interviewed in previous chapters were so disturbed by this idea that their entire birth plan was designed to *minimize* their chances of a C-section, for a huge chunk of American women, this kind of birth is their reality. And whether they choose to have a surgical birth or have the choice made for them by the circumstances of their pregnancy, they don't want your pity. While no one grows up dreaming about giving birth in an operating room, these women want you to know that a cesarean can be just as fulfilling and just as wonderful as a vaginal birth—and in some cases, they believe it can be even *better* for both mother and baby.

There is no question that the rate of cesarean sections has skyrocketed in the last few decades: In 1970, only 7 percent of American births were by C-section;[1] today that figure has zoomed to 29 percent.[2] You can hole yourself up in a library and spend months picking through the endlessly debated reasons for this development, but it basically comes

down to a confluence of trends, including the increasing age
of first-time mothers; the availability of safer, more routine
surgical procedures; the rise of purely elective C-sections;
the decline in vaginal births after cesareans (VBACs); the
evaporating veil of mystery over surgery itself (all those
TV makeover shows, with their close-ups of nose jobs and
liposuction, may have something to do with that); and a
fear of malpractice lawsuits, which may lead some doctors
to jump in with the scalpel when labor is progressing too
slowly for their comfort.

## A Long History

Cesarean sections have been around since, well, the days of Caesar, and they are even mentioned in ancient Chinese, Hindu, and Grecian folklore,[3] though moms generally didn't survive them in those days. Surgical births didn't become truly viable until the advent of anesthetics and antiseptics in the mid-nineteenth century. By 1901, 1 percent of all American babies were born via C-section.[4]

Both the World Health Organization (WHO) and the U.S. Department of Health and Human Services have gone so far as to declare a cesarean-section "epidemic," and have set a goal of keeping surgical births below 15 percent in developed countries and limited to instances in which the health of the mother or the child is at risk.[5,6] The interesting thing is how this statement has the innate ability to polarize women: Some see it as an important, vital movement for women to wrest control of their bodies back from scalpel-hungry and malpractice-phobic doctors; others hear the words "only if the mother's health is in danger" and cringe, because it rings uncomfortably close to the rhetoric spouted by anti-abortion activists. WHO's statement implies that the woman going under the knife is a passive victim of an aggressive doctor, when in fact many women are making the decision for themselves based on their own research and preferences. Just as they believe in the right to choose *whether* to have a baby, they believe in their absolute right to choose *how* to have it.

And while I have listened to women weep over their disappointment and sense of violation when they were wheeled in for an emergency C-section, I have listened to others describe the overwhelming relief they felt when they were told in advance that they were going to need one. Because there is a world of difference between a C-section that is done after hours of physically difficult labor and one that is performed before the mother has exhausted herself attempting a vaginal birth. And there is a huge emotional difference between a mother who has months or weeks to mentally prepare herself for a C-section and a mother who only has a couple of minutes to get used to the idea.

There's no doubt that an emergency C-section can be emotionally brutal and physically overwhelming, especially for a mom who has a specific, idealized childbirth scenario in her head (more about this in Chapter 11), but picture, if you will, a rather different situation: The mother is told weeks ahead of time that because of her health, the position of the baby, or other complicating factors, she is going to require a C-section. She reads up on the procedure and has plenty of time to mull over the fact that her baby will be born on her doctor's schedule, not Mother Nature's. She can call her family and tell them exactly when she will be going to the hospital; she can make arrangements for a sitter or Grandma to come take care of her older kids; she can hire a baby nurse and tell her the exact date she will need to arrive. She calmly checks into the hospital, where her relaxed, unrushed doctor performs the surgery, and a few hours later she is resting with her baby in her arms in the maternity ward. She has to take it easy for a few weeks, and may be on painkillers for a little while, but just like all her friends who had vaginal births, she comes home with a beautiful new baby. And she smiles to herself as her friends talk about unbearable labor pains or vaginal tears—things she never had to worry about.

For some women, this kind of narrative beats the unpredictable, uncontrollable alternative any day.

You may have read about the small but growing trend of women who choose C-sections with no urgent medical reason (and you can meet them in Chapter 10), but still, the vast majority of women who schedule surgical births do it because their doctor believes that the risks of a vaginal birth are too high.

There are numerous complications that can throw a hitch into your plans for a vaginal birth. If it is known ahead of time that the baby is breech (feet- or tush-down instead of head-down) or transverse (lying on his or her side), and your doctor or midwife is not able to turn the baby around manually by pushing on your abdomen, you will almost definitely be scheduled for a C-section. Babies who are in difficult positions *can* be born vaginally, and in fact have been born that way for centuries, but they do face a higher risk of injury from complications such as cord prolapse, when the umbilical cord slips out of the cervix before the baby and gets squeezed or pinched, cutting off the baby's air supply.[7] Your chances of needing a C-section also increase exponentially with the number of babies you're carrying. Because it is likely that at least one baby in a set of twins will be in an awkward position, around 50 percent of those deliveries are by C-section;[8] if you're having triplets or more, you can pretty much forget about any chance of having a vaginal birth (unless, of course, you live in the fictional world of *Friends*, where Phoebe easily delivered triplets vaginally while her wacky doctor hummed along to the theme song of *Happy Days*).

Other factors leading to a scheduled C-section could include a mother who has an outbreak of herpes or is HIV-positive; a mother who is showing signs of preeclampsia; a baby whose head appears to be too big to make it through the mother's pelvis; a complication such as placenta previa, in which the placenta is covering the opening of the cervix; or a baby whose amniotic fluid seems dangerously low or who shows signs of distress, making the doctor hesitant to risk a potentially long labor.

And then there's the complicated and controversial issue of repeat cesareans.

I remember talking to a friend of mine years ago, before I had kids, about the upcoming birth of her second child. "I'm scheduled for a C-section because I had one with my first son," she said. "I considered trying a vaginal birth this time, but when my doctor told me about the possibility of my uterus rupturing, I decided it was too risky." As she told me this, I had a mental image of my friend lying on a table while her entire middle section exploded into a cloud of dust, as if Wile E. Coyote had stuck one of those six-packs of dynamite in it.

*"I took a childbirth class for parents of twins. We watched a lot of movies of vaginal births, which only one out of ten of us wound up having. One movie was about a mom who didn't realize she was having triplets. She went on to give birth to all three babies unmedicated, moaning orgasmically the entire time. Most of us were laughing, and I remember remarking that if that were me in front of the camera, I'd have been screaming bloody murder."*

While the phrase "uterine rupture" still hits me like something out of a late-night horror flick, the reality isn't always quite so gruesome, and in fact uterine-rupture is pretty rare. It simply means that the incision made in the uterus during the first C-section begins to pull apart again. It could be a small and insignificant tear, noticed only in a postoperative exam, or it could be a catastrophic rupture, in which the mother loses blood, the baby's heart rate plummets, and he has to be removed immediately by C-section.

In the early days of C-sections, when doctors made a

long, vertical cut in the uterus, the risk of rupture during a VBAC was as high as 9 percent.[9] But now, most doctors use a lower, horizontal cut, which has a much smaller chance of splitting (a 2004 study in the *New England Journal of Medicine* that looked at 18,000 VBACs found that uterine ruptures occurred in less than 1 percent, which is much lower than the risk of needing an emergency C-section from other complications).[10] Having your labor induced with prostaglandins or oxytocin increases the risk of rupture,[11] as does previous uterine surgery and forceps- or vacuum-assisted delivery.[12]

Despite the relative safety of VBACs, over 300 hospitals have banned them,[13] and only 9 percent of women who had previous C-sections go on to give birth vaginally.[14] In fact, some of the women I interviewed believed that "once a C-section, always a C-section" was a law that no one would ever dare challenge. But many are simply so pleasantly surprised by their experience with the first C-section that they opt for a repeat performance, even if they don't have to: "When I was pregnant the second time, my doctor really downplayed the risks of a VBAC, so I wasn't afraid of that aspect," said Elise, a psychologist and mother of two in New York. "But my recovery was pretty easy with the first C-section, and I liked the idea that I could plan who would take care of my two-year-old and that I would know when to wrap up my work schedule, so I opted for another C-section."

Whatever the reason, there are hundreds of thousands of women every year who show up for an OB or midwife appointment sometime during their pregnancy, only to be told that their moment of childbirth is not going to unfold dramatically, with their water breaking, their partner timing contractions, and excited phone calls to surprised friends. Instead, it will be as prescripted as an infomercial for the George Foreman Grill. Instead of choosing between a birth center or a hospital, debating how far to go without drugs, and writing up a birth plan, they will be checking in for surgery.

For women who have been eagerly anticipating their labor and have specific ideas of how it will go, this news can be like a cold bucket of water poured over their warm and cuddly vision of how they will meet their child. There is a palpable sense of loss and disappointment. "When I found out that my daughter was breech and that I was going to have a C-section, I cried for days that I wasn't going to get to do it vaginally," said Julie, an artist and mother of two in New York. "I was scared about childbirth, but I was even more afraid of surgery—if I just cut my hand, I get lightheaded, and I was afraid I would feel them cutting me open. But most of all, I was upset that it was going to be so scheduled and technical. I really wanted that surprise of going into labor." As fate would have it, Julie's water broke five days before her scheduled surgery. "I called the doctor and he said, 'Don't worry, just walk over to the hospital and we'll do the C-section today.' So I got to feel some little contractions, but it never got to the point where it was really painful. I was actually quite thrilled that I got to have a 'natural' start to the labor."

What I heard most often from women who were told they would need C-sections was that after that initial wave of shock and disappointment, they moved on to acceptance and relief (and there were also women who skipped right over the disappointment phase and jumped right into *Thank god!*). Once these women realized that their birth was going to play out differently than they had imagined, they decided to look for some positives, and they found a surprisingly appealing silver lining.

"I had some complications with uterine fibroids, and perhaps because of that, my baby was stuck in the transverse position," explained Lisa, a design editor and mother of one in Scarsdale, New York. "My doctor told me I would probably need a C-section, though there was a chance the baby would turn at the last minute, in which case I could deliver vaginally. It was very difficult not knowing what was going to happen, so I kept weighing the pros and cons of each option, and I really was torn. On the one hand, you always see people in the movies and TV pushing, and I was a little disappointed I might not have the chance to try that." But when Lisa learned that the baby had not turned and she would need that C-section after all, she thought, *This might actually be good.* "I like planning things out," she explained. "I didn't have to worry about rushing to the hospital in the middle of the night, and I was able to get my hair done the day before. It was a very nice, controlled experience."

The fact that their baby's delivery date was predetermined—no waiting and pacing and then being surprised in the middle of the night—turned out to be an added bonus for many women, especially ones who had crazy work schedules or older kids. "I was able to schedule my last business meeting a couple days before the C-section, knowing that I wouldn't be sitting home for weeks on end with nothing to do," said Robin, a sales representative and mother of one in Milwaukee, Wisconsin. "Then, the night before the delivery, my husband and I went out for a very romantic dinner. By the next morning, I was ready to go."

And though they knew they might be trading off the pain of labor for some extra pain during recovery, many of these women were happy to do it. "I wasn't that concerned about pain from the surgery," said Elizabeth, a part-time caterer and mother of three in Portland, Oregon. "I was almost more afraid of natural childbirth, because of where the pain would be. It seems like if I'm going to have pain, I'd rather have it in my abdomen than down there!"

And using logic similar to that of women who opt for an epidural during vaginal birth, many of these women felt that eliminating the pain of labor meant they were more focused on the most important person in the room during the birth. "Since I was pain-free and didn't have to worry about things like torn tissue in my vagina, it was actually kind of fun," Stephanie told me. "I wasn't wrapped up in my own pain, and in a way that made me think more about the babies and less about myself."

Even though it is increasingly common and increasing numbers of women are choosing it, birth by cesarean section is still seen by most pregnant women as, at best, an unfortunate but lifesaving event and, at worst, a grueling, dehumanizing ordeal (this opinion comes mostly from the far left of the birth-choices continuum). Much of the concern I heard was about the mother becoming a passive participant in her own birth experience, and there was a lot of talk about the negative effect of a surgical birth on mother-baby bonding and breastfeeding. But the biggest fears and concerns were over submitting your body to such an invasive surgical procedure.

Among the increased risks to the mother from a cesarean section are infection, an adverse reaction to anesthesia (though since most C-sections are now done under epidural rather than general anesthesia, this is basically the same risk you take with any medicated birth), and excessive bleeding. There are also risks to the baby, including

*"I was fine with the scar. I never wore a bikini before the C-section, and I certainly didn't plan on wearing one after!"*

premature birth if the due date was not calculated correctly, a small risk of injury if the baby is nicked with the scalpel, and a greater incidence of breathing difficulties (babies born vaginally have the mucus naturally squeezed out of their lungs as they progress down the birth canal; C-section babies skip this part).

There is also a higher rate of maternal death from C-sections, though in the United States this occurrence is still very rare: only around 3.6 in 10,000 births, compared with 0.9 in 10,000 for all vaginal births.[15] But again, statistics do not tell the whole story. These figures include deaths from *all* cesarean births, including emergency ones, when the baby and mother are in danger before the doctor makes the first cut. Also, keep in mind that mothers who are at higher risk for bad outcomes because of advanced maternal age or preexisting health conditions are more likely to have a cesarean section, further affecting the numbers.

All the women I interviewed who had preplanned C-sections said they were informed of the risks by their doctors, but while some said they had extensive dialogues about it, others, like Robin, said, "My doctor told me there were risks with *any* surgery, but then in the same breath he explained how safe C-sections were and how many hundreds he had performed." When these women were told that a C-section was in the cards, many of them ran a Google search on the topic or ran over to Barnes & Noble to stock up on books about the procedure. But given the amount of time they had to process the idea, most showed up on the appointed day nervous but assured that everything would go fine. "I had a lot of confidence in my doctor, and C-sections are so common now that it didn't really frighten me," Lisa said. "In fact, it was such a controlled situation that in a way it seemed safer to me than a vaginal birth."

It also helped that everyone I spoke to could claim a sister, friend, or cousin who had gone through a successful C-section (they also liked to point out the many stories they heard of women who had long, complicated vaginal labors).

And the very fact that 29 percent of births are by C-section means that without a massive public policy change, the numbers are likely to keep going up—the more people you know with a healthy outcome of a C-section, the more likely you are to feel comfortable having one yourself. "When I found out I was going to have a C-section, my friends said, 'Go talk to people who've had them!' " said Julie. "And when I did, they all said, 'Oh, you're so lucky you know in advance! It'll be so easy.' And they were right."

No matter how many women tell you a scheduled C-section is a breeze, and no matter how speedy the operation is, a C-section is still major abdominal surgery. After the lower half of your body is numbed with an epidural and your abdomen is washed with an antibacterial solution, your doctor makes a small, horizontal incision above your pubic bone (this is often called a "bikini cut," because you can wear one again if you want to). When your doctor gets down to the uterus, she makes another low, horizontal cut, ruptures the amniotic sac, reaches in, and pulls out the baby. The cord is clamped and cut, and while the nurses or pediatricians suction out the baby's mucus and count the fingers and toes, your doctor removes your placenta and sews you back up. While it only takes a few minutes to get in, it can take a half hour to get back out.

I have heard several planned-C-section moms marvel at the round-headed cuteness of their newborns—since they have not been squished down the canal, they don't get that temporary conehead look that so many vaginally delivered babies are born with. In fact, a good friend of mine whose baby was born vaginally told me that when she was in the elevator bringing her new daughter home, a neighbor gave her what she considered the ultimate compliment: "That baby is so adorable, she must have been born by C-section!"

While most women said the surgery itself was painless (they frequently mentioned a dull sensation of being tugged), there were still plenty of complaints. One woman felt her stress level ratcheting up as her doctor argued loudly and aggressively with her anesthesiologist about the proper dosage of medication. A few women mentioned that as the doctor moved their insides around to get the best access to the baby, they suddenly felt unable to breathe. I heard accounts of severe nausea, intense vomiting, a sudden unquenchable thirst, and massive itching as the epidural wore off. Another mom was stunned when a nurse came into the recovery room and, without warning, pressed down hard on her newly stitched-up abdomen to squeeze out any excess air.

But for so many of these women, the very worst part of the whole operation was the epidural. When the first C-section mom I interviewed mentioned this to me, I responded, "Really? I thought the epidural was a piece of cake." And then I realized that I was in so much pain by the time I received the epidural that the actual injection was a welcome distraction—a slight sting that I knew would bring about unmitigated joy. But for a woman who arrives at the hospital feeling perfectly fine, and who has not yet felt even the tiniest flutter of a contraction, having a large needle stuck in her back can be a rather jarring and painful experience.

"Getting the epidural was horrible," said Paula, a mother of one in Columbus, Ohio. "That needle was just about as big as I could handle, and I cried through the whole thing. And getting the IV in my wrist was almost worse! The nurse seemed hurried, and it really hurt. After that, the surgery was easy."

Another disturbing aspect of the C-section for most of the moms was having their arms strapped down to the operating table. Besides the immediate feeling of being trapped, this also meant that the first cuddles with the new baby were pretty awkward. Yes, everyone mentioned the joyful moment when the doctor held up their new little son or daughter, and as soon as the baby was suctioned out and wrapped up, he or she was brought close to the mother's face for a peek and a nuzzle. C-section babies can't nurse immediately, which some women (and researchers) feel is crucial both for bonding and for getting breastfeeding off to a successful start.

Some women even confessed to me that they were afraid that if the baby was taken "unnaturally" from the womb, there might be some sort of emotional disconnect. "I was worried that my body wouldn't make the connection that she was mine," said Julie. "It did take a day or two for my milk to come in, but as far as bonding with her goes, there was no problem—I was in love from the second I saw her." And Lisa lamented, "I definitely wish I could have held him longer when I had the C-section. You can't really enjoy that moment so much. But I can't say it has affected our relationship. He is absolutely attached to me at the hip!"

While the dad or partner gets to follow the baby into the nursery, the C-section moms are steered into a recovery room, where they wait for the effects of the epidural to wear off and their body temperature to stabilize. It's not until they're moved to the maternity ward a few hours later that they are reunited with the baby and breastfeeding can begin. While some of the women I interviewed were disappointed that they didn't get to nurse right away, and a few believed it may have taken a bit longer for their milk to come in, everyone wound up breastfeeding within a few hours if that was their plan. I did find that this group of women, on average, nursed for less time than the women who had natural or medicated vaginal birth, but it's impossible to know whether that was due to the C-section, or whether both the type of birth and the length of time spent breastfeeding can be attributed to the mother's age, lifestyle, and personal preferences. But the fact is, the two women I know who breastfed their kids the longest—one is still going at four-and-a-half years—delivered their children by C-section.

In every book you read about pregnancy and childbirth, the author conscientiously reminds you that recovering from a surgical delivery is much harder than recovering from a vaginal birth (and hospital policies reflect this: women with vaginal deliveries are usually sent home after two days, while C-section moms stay for four). But all the moms I interviewed for this chapter, all of which had preplanned C-sections, felt that they had a far easier recovery period than they would have had they pushed for hours before going in for surgery. They generally felt that would have resulted in a double dose of vaginal stretching *and* incisional pain, and many even argued that they were *less* exhausted and beat-up than women who had gone through long labors ending in vaginal delivery.

While they definitely talked about being sore at the site of the incision ("Even five years later, I occasionally feel a little twinge," one mom told me), having a hard time getting in and out of bed, and keeping up a steady dose of painkillers, a few of the women were able to walk around comfortably by the next day. "After the first day, all I needed was some ibuprofen to make me comfortable," said Rita, a pharmacist and mother of two in Chicago. "I did not experience that feeling of being run over by a truck that I've heard women describe after long labors."

It also helps that women who undergo C-sections are under doctor's orders to take it easy for the first couple of weeks. "I think that, in a way, I healed faster, or at least more efficiently, from the C-section than from the vaginal birth because my doctor ordered me to stay in bed for two weeks and instructed my husband to treat me like a queen," said Jennie, who had a C-section six years after a vaginal birth with her first child. "With the first birth, I was really beat-up down there from four hours of pushing and having my doctor's arm up inside me. But since it was a vaginal birth, I had the idea that I should be able to just get back on my feet. I wish the doctor had told me to stay in bed for two weeks the first time!"

No matter how satisfied you may be with your C-section, everywhere you look, a childbirth pundit or even another mom is giving you some not-so-subtle hints that a surgical birth is not "natural," that it is a second-rate experience, that it detracts from your power as a woman. And no matter how entrenched that baby was in her sideways pose or how serious the complications may have been, there can still be a lingering sense that somehow you failed to get the job done. "I sense from some people that they are embarrassed about having to have a C-section," said Marin, a librarian and mother of twins in Cortlandt Manor, New York. "I don't get it. It's not like you did something wrong if your baby is breech or your labor doesn't progress."

Books that describe unmedicated vaginal birth as the ultimate experience of womanhood and childbirth classes that focus on breathing and birthing positions—with just a brief discussion of C-sections—don't make it any easier. "I read a couple of books and took a Lamaze class, all of which assumed that I would want to and be able to have an unmedicated vaginal birth," Stephanie told me. "A C-section was seen as something that the doctors would try to manipulate me into doing and that I should avoid at all costs. The class basically set us up to make us feel like we missed out. I even interviewed a doula who my friend loved, and all she did was proselytize about natural birth. I felt that she was implying that if I *did* have a C-section, even though I was carrying twins, I was not trying hard enough. It pissed me off and also made me aware of how judgmental the whole birthing thing is."

Since all the women in this chapter had compelling medical reasons to have a C-section, they didn't experience very much blatant criticism, but they did have to deal with friends who bit their lips, cocked their heads, and said, "Ohhh, are you okay?" And when you have just been through the joyous experience of becoming a mom—no matter what the technical details—the last thing you want to hear is, "Sorry, that must have been awful." "I had people feeling sorry for me, thinking it must have been so horrible and so painful, and that was not true at all!" said Rita. "I just didn't understand why they would react that way." Another mom told me that her coworkers at a health-food co-op never once asked how her scheduled C-section for her breech baby went, yet they had no problem extending loads of compassion to another mom whose birth-center experience turned into a trip to the emergency room.

But really, what many of these women felt, rather than being victimized or distraught, was a huge sense of relief that they were able to take some sort of control over the *outcome* of their situation, even if it meant handing over control of the actual birth experience to their doctor. There would be no frantic gurney rides in the middle of the night as teams of doctors rushed to get the baby out before he ran out of oxygen. They wouldn't have to worry about the baby getting stuck halfway down the exit ramp and then refusing to budge any more. It's definitely a trade-off—lying down on an operating table under a fluorescent lamp is no one's idea of a "gentle" birth—but like the women who choose medicated birth over natural birth, these women all said they were more focused on the outcome of the birth than on the process. They believed in their doctor, they believed in the system, and they believed that they were giving their baby the safest, healthiest entrance into the world.

"With my first child, I had an emergency C-section after thirteen hours of labor, and I felt so sad that I couldn't have a vaginal birth. I felt like I had failed," said Kara, a stay-at-home mother of two in Great Neck, New York. "When I had my second child four years later, I went past my due date and the doctor was worried that there was a risk of uterine rupture if she got too large. And I didn't really want to go through a long labor, only to wind up in an emergency C-section again. So I went in for a planned C-section. That one was so easy, it was like the reward for the difficulty of the first one. I had no pain during the delivery, and barely any after the medication wore off. It was a cakewalk. And I came to the realization that the childbirth experience, while miraculous and beautiful, is really a tiny speck in the experience of parenthood. How the child got here is pretty insignificant compared to how he or she is guided through life."

## CHAPTER TEN

# MY BABY, MY BELLY, MY DECISION: MATERNAL-CHOICE C-SECTION

*O*ne of the reasons I waited until I was thirty-seven to have a baby was that I was terrified of childbirth. *When I got pregnant, I thought,* Okay, I'll deal with that when I get there. *But still, the more I learned about it in childbirth classes and in books, the more nervous I got. When I was about seven months pregnant, a friend of mine told me she had had an elective C-section. She described how quickly it went, what a rapid recovery she had afterward, and how nontraumatic the birth was for her son—his Apgar scores were 10 and 10. She was also very frank about what a relief it was not to have to worry about an episiotomy or tearing or incontinence, or whether sex would ever be enjoyable again. As soon as she told me about it, I knew instantly that it was what I wanted to do. I was on pins and needles until my next OB appointment, but when I asked* *my doctor if he would perform an elective C-section, he agreed right away.*

*My surgery was scheduled for a Sunday morning in September. The hospital was far busier when I arrived than expected, but I was finally wheeled into the operating room a couple hours behind schedule, and things happened very quickly from there. My OB held me while I got the epidural, and then at 12:12 PM, he announced he was going to start. I couldn't see what was going on, but I could hear a lot of rustling and felt some tugging. I also smelled a burning odor, which confused me, until I realized the doctor was cauterizing. The surgery was quick—at 12:20 PM, the doctor held my son up, and he absolutely took my breath away. It was the most amazing moment. Getting sewn up took some more time, but I was focused solely on seeing what was going on with my little guy and hearing his first cries. I was really happy with how it turned out, and if I decide to have another child, I would absolutely do it again.*

**EILEEN, COMPUTER CONSULTANT**

**AND MOTHER OF ONE**

*Rego Park, New York*

The first time I ever heard about a completely elective, non-emergency C-section, I was seven or eight months pregnant with my second child. I had just hired a new baby sitter to watch my almost-two-year-old daughter a couple of days a week. Lena was from Ecuador, and she had the long blond hair and golden glow of someone who spent a lot of time at the beach (which she did), and the snappy speech of a bright, opinionated college student (which she was). One day she was sitting at the kitchen table, feeding Bellamy lunch as I got ready to go to my OB appointment. "Why don't you just go in for a C-section? It's like *zip-zip,* and you're done, no problem," she said to me, slicing through the air with a spoonful of yogurt for effect.

*"What?"* I replied. "There's no reason for me to have a C-section. This is a perfectly healthy pregnancy! Why would I put myself under the knife for major surgery if I don't have to?"

"Everybody I know does it," Lena explained. "It's so much easier. Why would you want to go through all that pain if you don't have to? And you know, it stretches you out down there. Yuck. This way, you're in and out, and it's nothing—you don't even see the scar. My mother had all of us that way."

I left for my appointment shaking my head at Lena's youthful ignorance, and I'm sure she clucked to her friends about how silly these American women are, suffering through all that pain and agony when they could just go in for a quick procedure and be out at the beach in a bikini a week or two later.

A month or two later, I gave birth to my second daughter vaginally, and a week or two after that, Lena decided her calling in life was to be a travel agent rather than a nanny. But our conversation stuck with me, and I thought of her again when I was researching this book and discovered that in some South American countries (particularly Brazil), the C-section rate for affluent women in private hospitals can be as high as 60 to 90 percent.[1]

Lena's blasé attitude about C-sections—she seemed to think they were no more risky or painful than an eyebrow waxing—could be attributed to cultural differences and the absolute certainty about life that only a twenty-year-old could possess. But what was I to think when I started asking around and found that several women I knew—highly educated, smart, sophisticated women who were devoted mothers—also chose to bypass vaginal birth for a pre-planned, completely elective C-section? These were women whose judgment I absolutely respected in so many other aspects of parenting. They weren't twenty years old. They didn't do it on a whim. They weren't selfish or ignorant. There had to be a lot more to this idea than I had thought that day in my kitchen when I balked at Lena's suggestion.

In the last couple of years, elective C-section has become one of those topics that magazines and news organizations love to jump on—it's easy to illustrate with candid pictures of pregnant celebrities (hello, Britney Spears!) and it's instantly combustible. Just put it out there and watch as another battle in the Mommy Wars sparks into action. When Victoria "Posh Spice" Beckham gave birth to her son Brooklyn via C-section in 1999, the British tabloids couldn't resist the perfect head-line: Too Posh to Push. Plenty of other boldface moms who've elected to have C-sections, such as Madonna, Claudia

Schiffer, Elizabeth Hurley, and Denise Richards, have helped keep the trend in the news (though it's difficult to cut through the PR spin and tell which ones were truly elective).

In 2003, Fox News even ran a piece suggesting that women were choosing C-sections to avoid late-pregnancy stretch marks[2]—which is ridiculous, considering you'd have to have your C-section in your second trimester for this to really work. And when a mother-to-be on one of those ubiquitous childbirth reality shows announced that she wanted a C-section because vaginal birth was "barbaric," *"The surgery was a breeze, and because I didn't go through extensive labor, I had a lot of energy left, so I was truly alert and delighted when I saw my child."* message boards all over the web lit up with women excoriating her "idiotic" beliefs.

Slowly but surely, the women who choose C-sections are starting to fight back. On blogs and online magazines, they are explaining, sometimes angrily, and always passionately, that the decision about whether to have a child vaginally or surgically is theirs to make. They are going into this choice fully informed and completely in control. They are doing what they think is best and safest for themselves and their baby. They want the ~~critics~~ you to send their guilt trips somewhere else.

The way the media has painted this picture, you would think that millions of women were lining up at hospitals, swiping their credit cards, and asking if they can be out in time for their manicure appointment at noon. But while elective C-section is a growing trend, it is still a relatively small slice of the childbearing pie: In 2002, an estimated 2.5 percent of all births were elective C-sections, up 25 percent from just two years earlier.[3] It's not a huge amount, but it's still more than twice the combined number of women who give birth at home or in independent childbirth centers. Still, it is hard to get a real sense of the numbers, since doctors don't necessarily reveal when a C-section is elective, and conversely, many births that are planned as C-sections would have inevitably turned into emergency C-sections if they were attempted vaginally.

And though home-birth moms and elective-C-section moms would seem to have absolutely nothing in common— one side strives for the least medical, most mom-centric birth; the other chooses the least natural, most doctor-centric birth—I found an astounding number of similarities between these two seemingly diametrically opposed groups. First and foremost, both groups are criticized by mainstream moms as selfish and irrational. Other women hear about these types of births and make assumptions about the women's motivations that are often completely off the mark. In fact, I found that some of the most outspoken critics of elective C-sections and home births alike had never even talked to anyone who had deliberately made either choice.

Are there women who choose to have a C-section simply because they can't be bothered with the inconvenience of a vaginal birth? Possibly. Though if convenience is all you want, you can always pick a date to induce vaginally, and since you are required to both stay in the hospital longer and recuperate at home longer for a C-section than for a vaginal birth, it's not as if you can be off to your tennis game the next day. Are there women who choose a C-section *solely* because they think it is unladylike to scream and grunt and then shoot a baby out of your vagina? There may be, but I didn't meet them.

Again, just like the home-birth women I met, the women who chose C-sections did it because they felt, *in their particular case,* that it was the safest, healthiest, most empowering option. Most of these women were over thirty-five—some were over forty—when they had their first child (in the medical literature, this group is tagged with the humiliating term "geriatric mothers"), and they knew that the odds of ending up with a C-section even after putting forth their most valiant effort at a vaginal birth were uncomfortably high. So instead of passively waiting until they or the baby were in distress, they preferred to take charge of the situation and plan a *nonemergency* C-section, which has a lower risk of complications and an easier recovery than a C-section after attempted vaginal birth. In fact, a study in the *British Medical Journal* in 2005 found that almost 20 percent of all first-time mothers over thirty-four who had no medical complications chose to have a C-section anyway.[4]

"I was forty-four when I had my son, and I found out that women my age had a much higher risk of placenta previa and a more than 40 percent chance of having a C-section," explained Marie , a former lawyer and mother of one in New York. "My doctor also had her first child after she was forty, and she had gone through a very difficult labor, so when I asked about a scheduled C-section, she thought it was a wise idea. I think instead of romanticizing the idea of childbirth, I just looked at it in a very logical way, and this made the most sense. My partner had seen her sister go through a very painful birth process, so she completely supported my plan."

## Safety in Small Numbers

If you're planning on sprouting your own little softball team, think twice about scheduling a C-section. Since each successive surgery leaves the uterus more prone to a rupture, doctors generally recommend that elective C-sections only be done on women who plan to have no more than one or two children.

In addition to being older and having invested more years in their careers, I found that these women were more practical in their visions of motherhood. They talked about the thrill of seeing their babies for the first time and the love they felt for them, but no one talked about motherhood as the ultimate fulfillment of her lifelong journey to womanhood.

There is no question that the desire to eliminate the pain of labor was a huge factor in these decisions, but it was more about the fact that in so many of the cases these women had heard about, the pain had no payoff: Their friends, coworkers, or cousins struggled and stretched and pushed and ended up with difficult and unsatisfying births anyway. "Three of my friends had babies just before I did, and they all told me these horrible delivery stories where they were in labor for nineteen or twenty hours," said Ellen, a small-business owner and mother of two in Goldsboro, North Carolina. "One baby had the cord wrapped around his neck, another one had it around his abdomen, and they did all kinds of pushing, and the baby's heartbeat went down, and they wound up having emergency C-sections. A couple of them told me they were crying for their doctor to go ahead and do a C-section earlier on, but the doctors were very unsympathetic. Everyone turned out fine, but I thought, *There is no way I am going through that.*"

While I was listening to the elective-C-section moms tell these dramatic stories about their friends' emergency C-sections (plus, to a lesser degree, tales of painful episiotomies and heartless doctors), I had a weird sense of déjà vu: *Where have I heard this before?*

Yes, of course. It was back when I was interviewing home-birth and birth-center moms. Women in all these gourps were rattled by stories of moms who lost control of the situation, who wound up dazed, exhausted, and emotionally blindsided by a birth that started out in the delivery room and ended up on the operating table. It was how they processed this information and then acted on it that made all the difference: Based on all those life factors that make up one's childbirth persona—feelings about doctors, pain, and one's body; political, religious, and philosophical beliefs—and whether they blamed the failure of the vaginal birth on nature or on medical interference, these women reacted either by opting out of the hospital altogether, or by spinning around in the opposite direction and saying, *Damn it! If I'm going to have a C-section anyway, I want to do it on my own terms.*

Here's something to think about: While most people assume that a C-section—major surgery in which a doctor cuts you open and moves your insides around—is by definition much more abusive to your body than giving birth the "natural" way, there is a growing body of research suggesting that over the long run, an elective C-section might actually be the *gentler* choice. These studies look at the long-term effects of a vaginal delivery on the condition of a woman's pelvic floor and have concluded that women who deliver vaginally have a higher rate of incontinence, uterine prolapse (when the pelvic floor becomes so weak that the uterus winds up dangling into the vagina), and bladder problems[5] (though a 2005 study in *Obstetrics & Gynecology* that looked at 143 pairs of sisters suggested that genetics played a bigger part in determining the risk of pelvic-floor problems than a history of vaginal delivery did).[6]

While much of this research is still somewhat controversial, the potential pain and discomfort of dealing with pelvic-floor problems years after any C-section incisions would have healed is enough to convince many moms to go for the surgical alternative—especially moms who have seen the problems up close. "As a urogynecologist, I couldn't see myself going through labor and possibly having to face all those problems later in life," says Stacey, a physician and mother of two in St. Louis. "I see women years after they've had seemingly uneventful deliveries who have terrible pro-lapse, overactive bladders, and urinary incontinence. When people talk about a C-section as if it is a worst-case scenario, I have to wonder if they know the scientific literature. I feel like I preserved my pelvic floor, and that will offer me a better quality of life."

Now, while no one would ever think about using images of urinary incontinence and organs protruding into the vagina as bedroom talk, I found that the conversation about elective C-sections does inevitably turn to sex. Doctors and scientists use technical terms like "vaginal integrity" to talk about post-childbirth intercourse, but it all comes down to this: How are you going to want to get your groove on again after your vagina has been stretched, torn, or snipped?

"I had heard several stories from new-mom friends of mine—and read more online—about how post-baby sex could be unpleasant, embarrassing, and painful," said Donna, a stay-at-home mother of one from Spokane, Washington. "But with a planned C-section, I knew I would be able to return to having sex without any physical problems. I was actually surprised to find out that women who have C-sections are supposed to wait six weeks, the same as for vaginal births. It's not like

## But What Do the Doctors Think?

In a 2005 survey of more than 300 recently trained ob-gyns, two-thirds said they would perform an elective C-section on a first-time mom if the patient wished to avoid the possibility of future pelvic-floor disorders.[7]

we had the date marked on the calendar and were counting down the days, but we started having sex again right around that six-week mark and there were no problems at all."

I got the sense from talking to these women that opting for an elective C-section is a little like joining a secret society. It is a choice that is rarely discussed in the mainstream pregnancy books—it's still treated as a newsworthy oddity—and if you don't have any complications that would make vaginal delivery a risky proposition, your doctor is not going to say, "Hey, maybe you should consider surgery just for the heck of it." You have to come upon the idea on your own.

Some women researched the facts and then tentatively brought up the idea to their doctor, having no idea whether or not this kind of thing was even allowed. Others heard about the procedure through the pregnancy grapevine. Apparently, women in coffee shops and at baby showers all over America are pulling aside their friends and whispering in their ears: "Guess what I did? And you can do it, too."

"I wish elective C-sections got more visibility so more women could know that it is a legitimate choice," said Kyra, a teacher and mother of one in Pittsburgh, who first heard about elective C-sections through a cousin.

What you wind up with is a childbirth choice that is akin to the chef's off-the-menu special—it's back there in the kitchen, but you have to know to ask for it. And while it is each doctor's prerogative whether to perform the surgery or not, the American College of Obstetricians and Gynecologists (ACOG) stated in 2003 that if a patient is fully informed of the risks involved in a C-section, has discussed various alternative options, and has made some attempt to address any lingering fears about childbirth, then her doctor can ethically grant her request for a C-section or refer her to another doctor who will.[8]

This stance has, of course, been assailed by natural-birth advocates and those who believe the rate of C-sections is unconscionably high. A 2004 article in *Mothering* magazine, for example, insisted that women who opt for elective C-sections are misinformed and succumbing to pressure from their doctors and the media.[9] But for these moms, having someone pat them on the head and say, "You can't possibly be making an educated decision; we'll tell you the right thing to do," is infuriating. Many of their responses can be summed up like this: If that mom over there can read all the literature by natural-birth advocates and come to the conclusion that a home birth is best for her, then how dare you question my ability to analyze the data and decide that a C-section is the best choice for me?

Even though ACOG has given patient-choice C-sections a qualified nod of approval (the party line is that it should be requested by the patient, not offered by the doctor), it does not mean that getting one is always as easy as calling up the hospital and picking a date for surgery. Interestingly, while some natural-birth advocates paint a picture of lawsuit-fearing doctors ready to grab the knife at the first opportunity, some of the women I spoke with tried everything they could to coerce their doctor to pull out his scalpel. Ellen told me that her doctor refused to consider an elective C-section, even though she brought it up at several appointments. Finally, in the last weeks of her pregnancy, she forced the issue by paying out of her own pocket for a last-minute sonogram. "I thought my only chance of getting the C-section I wanted was if the baby was breech," she explained. "He was convinced I only wanted the sonogram to get a peek at the sex of the baby."

To Ellen's great relief, the baby was indeed turned the wrong way, and she got her wish for a preplanned C-section. Had she not insisted on that sonogram, Ellen is certain she would have gone through several hours of pointless vaginal labor before her doctor would have decided to perform the surgery.

Even when your doctor is cool with your decision, you may have to jump through some other frustrating hoops, as Marie discovered: "The hospital was uncomfortable with the idea of an elective C-section, and they insisted that I have a consultation with a psychiatrist first," she explained. "I thought that was totally intrusive, since it's my body and I should be able to make a decision about what kind of birth I want. But I understand that the hospital has to report to the state about their rate of C-sections, and I guess they wanted to prove that I was of sound mind and it was completely my choice. In the end, it wasn't that big a deal, and my insurance paid for the shrink appointment, but I definitely would have preferred not to have done it."

Home births and elective C-sections, while polar opposites in so many ways, are united in the unmitigated amount of criticism that women get for having them. Whereas the decision about whether to go natural or medicated *within* a hospital generally elicits a reaction of, "Well, I wouldn't do that, but to each her own," the decision to jump way out of the mainstream on either side of the childbirth spectrum is seen as a slap in the face to public decency. When I asked women with more socially accepted birth choices what they thought of elective C-sections, I had to stand back as voices thundered, teeth clenched, and the caps lock keys on their computers stayed firmly pressed. "Scheduling an unnecessary C-section is TOTALLY insane" was one of the typical responses I received. "It's lazy, crazy, and cruel."

A good deal of the criticism is over the perceived insanity of choosing to be cut open, of submitting oneself to an emergency procedure that was developed with the express purpose of saving babies and moms who otherwise would have died. "I can't understand how any sane woman would undergo abdominal surgery when she could give birth the way God designed us," a natural-birth mom told me via email. "No one can claim that a C-section is equally as safe as a vaginal birth, not to mention the mother is going to miss out on an incredible experience."

But the most damning judgment came down on the supposed inability of these women to be decent, caring, selfless mothers. "Childbirth is not meant to be convenient or easy or sanitized!" said a mother of two. "If you can't go through a little discomfort and a little effort and leave a few things up to fate, like the time and date of your child's birth, how good a parent are you going to be?" Another mom confessed, "I imagine this woman handing the baby off to a sitter on day one and then being on her merry way."

There is an assumption made that the mother is putting her own interests—her fear of pain, her desire for a controlled experience—ahead of the best interests of the baby, which is roughly the equivalent of accusing these mothers of being flesh-eating, puppy-smothering cyborgs. But C-section moms will come right back at you with vivid tales of babies who were stuck in the birth canal too long, who were deprived of oxygen and permanently damaged, all in the name of vaginal birth. Some will argue that by protecting the baby from the trauma of vaginal birth, they are actually giving her a better, healthier entrance into the world— and they will quote their stellar Apgar scores to prove it. (Though a 2006 study of more than six million births concluded that there is a somewhat higher rate of neonatal mortality for low-risk selective C-sections—1.7 deaths per 1,000 deliveries compared to 0.62 for all vaginal births.)[10]

*"Someone once said to me, 'Giving birth naturally is the ultimate expression of womanhood.' Well, it's true that men can't do it, but they can't give birth by C-section, either."*

But for those who are incensed that a mother can't suffer through some pain and unpredictability for the sake of her child, I have to ask this: Can you completely separate the needs of the mother from the needs of the child? Isn't a baby best served by a mother who is happy and satisfied with her birth experience? Yes, for many women, having a vaginal birth is going to be the most beautiful and empowering experience, but for a whole lot of sane, sensitive, well-meaning moms, it just isn't. And forcing them to go through one because the majority believes it is the morally superior way to give birth is just as oppressive as forcing someone to have an unnecessary C-section.

"I got the feeling other moms thought I was selling out," said Marie "They would talk about vaginal birth as if it were the brass ring, and say that a C-section was somehow less motherly and less legitimate. But I didn't let it faze me. My pregnancy was wonderful, and my delivery was easy—I was on my feet the next day and was able to take care of the baby and breastfeed him right away. It was definitely the right choice for me, and it helped that I had the complete support of my doctors, my partner, and my family."

Not everyone is quite as lucky, however. Just like those home-birth moms, several of the elective-C-section moms felt they had to keep their plans under wraps, lest anyone try to talk them out of it. "I was worried that my family and friends wouldn't be supportive," said Carmen, a mother of one in Brooklyn. "I have a lot of fairly crunchy friends, and I had heard them talk about how they didn't want to 'medicalize' their birth experience. At my baby shower, I brought up the idea of an elective C-section casually, saying it was an option I had heard about, and my friends said, 'Oh, but you wouldn't really want to do that!' We didn't tell any relatives because we were worried about their reactions, and that was a real disappointment. My sister was very negative about the whole idea. I would have loved to talk to her about it, but I felt I couldn't."

Clearly, an elective C-section is not the right choice for everyone. Despite my feelings about pain during labor, I would still choose a vaginal birth over a C-section. But clearly no choice is right for everyone—not home births, birth-center births, or medicated vaginal births. Though there seems to be a general assumption that a surgical birth is always emotionally and medically inferior to a vaginal one, keep in mind that almost all the studies on the aftereffects of C-sections have been done on women *who didn't want one*. Yes, when a woman's vision of her ideal childbirth experience is snatched away from her by complications, a pushy doctor, or insurance concerns, it can be tragic, and it can affect her feelings as a mother (see Chapter 11). But when a woman makes the decision *herself* to have a C-section, after she's examined all the medical data and discussed it with her doctor, and upon deep reflection has found that it is the one spot on the childbirth spectrum that will make her feel in control and excited to have her baby, then it really can be the right thing for her to do. "My C-section was such a positive experience for me," said Eileen. "I think it's important for such a personal choice to be honored and for women to have every opportunity to learn about the different options and decide for themselves."

## CHAPTER ELEVEN

# EXPECT *the* UNEXPECTED: WHEN LABOR DOESN'T GO *as* PLANNED

When I waddled into the New York University Medical Center on those two sticky July nights in 2001 and 2003, the only hazy, half-baked birth plan I had was that I wanted an epidural, and I wanted to deliver vaginally. That was it. I had no opinions about Pitocin, about labor positions, about who should cut the cord, or how soon I should hold the baby. And both times, I got what I wanted: two uncomplicated vaginal births, a miraculously effective epidural, and two healthy baby girls.

In that small but not insignificant way, my birth story shares a common thread with almost all of the others you have read about so far in this book. Just like Charlotte, who gave birth in her bathtub at home, and like Eileen, who checked in for an elective C-section, and everyone in between, I chose a method of childbirth, followed through with it, and was happy with the results. The degree of mothers' satisfaction varied, of course: Some moms were ecstatic, while others were simply relieved and content. Save for a few details that they felt could have played out better (a painful IV insertion here, an insensitive nurse there), they basically had no regrets.

Unfortunately, not every story ends that way.

All you have to do is log on to one of the web's many postpartum message boards to get a sense of the million little things that can go wrong during labor: questionable decisions made in the heat of the moment; unforeseen complications with your health or your baby's health that can escalate into bigger things, which can, in turn blow up into an emergency situation that tramples all over that ideal birth scenario you had been sketching out in your mind for the past eight or nine months. Sometime during your labor, a doctor or midwife might make a suggestion that points you down a different path than the one you had hoped to travel. Your baby can refuse to budge in a timely manner, or your body might refuse to play along properly, and before you have a minute to rethink your plan, you wind up getting induced, accepting the epidural, transferring to the hospital, or lying on an operating table, saying, *This is not at all how I wanted this to go.*

No matter what your politics are, what you think of the state of medical care today, or how much effort you put into planning your baby's birth, your labor may wind up being one of the unpredictable, uncontrollable, difficult ones.

Consider an acquaintance of mine, one of the most passionate advocates of natural birth I know, who prepared for her labor as if she were gearing up to compete in a triathlon while defending her PhD dissertation. Despite all her hard work, she developed signs of preeclampsia and had to be induced early in a hospital. (She did get the "gentle birth" she wanted, assisted by a midwife, but the circumstances surrounding it made her so angry and tense that her labor stalled at one point.)

Now compare that to the experience of another woman I interviewed, who was so afraid of childbirth that she planned an elective C-section and did zero preparation for birth. Yet when her water broke early and her labor come on too quickly to make it into surgery, she had a fast, easy vaginal delivery that she proclaimed, "wasn't as bad as I expected." It just goes to show you that while passion and preparation go a long way toward shaping your birth experience, so does your underlying health, your age, your environment, and ultimately some ineffable form of childbirth fate that just doesn't care what the hell you think or want.

Because crazy and unfortunate things happen. Ten to 15 percent of births that start out at home or in a birth center are transferred to a hospital. Labor can last for days on end. Babies get stuck. Moms develop high blood pressure and diabetes. Even in the World Health Organization's best-case scenario, 15 percent of babies would still need to be delivered by C-section. In the United States, even in the twenty-first century, a small percentage of babies will get injured on the way out, and sometimes even die. (Since the trauma of dealing with a sick baby is a whole other topic for a whole other book, though, I am limiting my discussion to births that didn't go as planned but still resulted in healthy babies.)

This isn't to say you should just throw up your hands, leave everything to the whims of the childbirth gods, and hope for the best. Not at all. The unpredictability of childbirth is even *more* of a reason to educate yourself and prepare the best you can. Because when you arrive at a crossroads where your baby's birth can go one way or another, when the doctor or midwife is hovering over you, questioning whether to manually break your water or to try a narcotic to "take the edge off the pain," being prepared and knowing what you want is your best possible defense against letting your labor veer off in a completely different direction.

And sometimes all that education and preparation will be enough. But sometimes it just won't. So while you're gearing yourself up, make sure you keep an itsy-bitsy, tiny little window in your mind open to the idea that things might not go as planned. Because the more adamant you are that there is only one perfect scenario for delivering this baby—that anything else will be second-rate—the more devastated you will be when it doesn't happen. And you are going to blame someone. It might be your doctor, it might be your midwife or your husband, or it might be yourself.

When I was pregnant with my first daughter, I can't remember expending any mental energy on what would happen if

I needed a C-section. I was healthy; I was only thirty-three, which is practically a teenager in Manhattan Mom years. I had no complications with my pregnancy, and my doctor estimated that my baby would be on the small side (she was right—Bellamy was a smidge under six pounds). So there was no indication that a surgical birth was in the cards for me. Having read an excerpt from Naomi Wolf's book *Misconceptions*, which included her gruesome description of watching her own emergency C-section in the reflection of a glass door in the operating room, I knew I preferred not to have one, but it seemed to be one of those remote possibilities that only happened to other people. I flipped right past those chapters in the pregnancy books.

Boy, was I naive. Knowing now that the odds of giving birth by C-section are almost one in three, and having spoken to so many women who had perfectly unremarkable pregnancies, only to be rushed in for surgery at the last minute, I realize how incredibly lucky I was to have avoided a C-section. I also realize how incredibly unprepared I would have been had it happened.

Unlike women who have *planned* C-sections, who have the luxury of time to digest the information, weigh the pros and cons, and get advice and reassurance from other moms, women who have emergency C-sections may have only a few minutes to absorb what is happening to them. Though some women say their primary emotion was relief that their long labor would finally be over, others felt a mixture of fear, anxiety, and dismay when they were told they were heading for surgery. Those emotions, combined with the exhaustion they felt from hours of labor, left them in a complete daze—not the best condition in which to mentally prepare for surgery. In one study of the psychological reverberations of different methods of childbirth, women who had emergency C-sections reported having the most negative birth experience, followed by women who had forceps- or vacuum-assisted delivery, and both groups showed a higher rate of postpartum depression than women who had preplanned C-sections or normal vaginal deliveries.[1]

"I wish I had had more information about C-sections so it wouldn't have been so frightening," said Sally, a mom in Nashville, Tennessee, who was induced ten days after her due date and then labored for thirteen hours with a baby who was in an awkward position and refused to descend. "I hadn't had surgery since a tonsillectomy when I was four. When they strapped my arms down, I felt like I was being crucified, and the operating room was so cold and sterile compared to the warm and pretty labor room I had just been in, with its stereo and hardwood floors. The whole experience was just shocking."

That shock—and the feeling that whatever control they might have had before has just slipped irretrievably through their fingers—is the worst for women who planned to have natural, unmedicated births. For many of them, the idea of an epidural, or even an IV, is unwanted and invasive, and now not only are they stuck with both of those, they are also having the mother of all interventions, a surgical birth. "I had wanted to do everything natural," said Naomi, a lawyer in Phoenix who had a C-section after laboring unsuccessfully for hours. "Before I got pregnant with Annie, I had had surgery to remove a ruptured fallopian tube, and all through the childbirth classes, I kept telling my husband, 'Whatever you do, don't let them cut me open again.' I remember lying there on the operating table, looking up at the lights and thinking, *This cannot be happening to me.*"

When these moms recalled the stress and anxiety they felt as they were prepped for surgery, I couldn't help but compare it to the casual, optimistic atmosphere many of the moms who had undergone preplanned C-sections described. Most planned C-sections are preventive—the doctor is choosing to take the baby out *before* there is distress. But when you have been pushing for a while or the baby's heart rate is declining and your doctor tells you that it will be safer to get the baby out *right now* by surgery, rather than letting the baby spend another minute inside, the thought that goes through every mom's head is, *Oh my god, is the baby going to make it?* Everything you have hoped for in a lifetime of baby dreams, and even maybe years of trying

*"The biggest challenge is getting over my scar. I had never had any surgery, and my body had never been marred before. It plays out when we're being intimate, I'm trying to be sexy, and there's this big scar over my crotch! My husband is great about it. He says, 'That's the mark of our baby!' But it's getting lighter and lighter every day."*

to get pregnant, and nine months of getting to know the creature inside of you seems as if it might vanish in an instant.

"At one point during my labor, I was lying back, listening to the *beep beep beep* of the fetal monitor, and suddenly, the beeps started slowing down," recalled Naomi. "I freaked out, and a nurse ran in and threw an oxygen mask over my face. She stabilized the baby pretty quickly, but it scared me to death. I was thinking, *I have not waited this long to have a baby just to have her die on me.* Soon after that, I went into active labor. I pushed for almost an hour, and the baby was not even crowning. I was sure she was being traumatized by being stuck in the canal, and I didn't want her to suffer any longer, so when the doctor suggested a C-section, I agreed. When you think your baby's life is in danger, getting her out safely is the only thing on your mind."

Whether it's via C-section, with forceps, with more pain than you had expected, or with an epidural or an internal monitor you didn't want, somehow that baby gets out, and soon the mom is in the maternity ward or back home, getting to know her new child. No matter what the details of the birth, if the baby is healthy, there is a huge sense of relief and thankfulness.

But for moms whose birth experience was not what they planned, the joy and relief is often mixed in with a sense of disappointment and sadness, made even more complicated by the standard hormonal mishmash of baby blues. Many moms expressed a sense of loss over being denied the beautiful experience of childbirth they had read and heard so much about.

Much of this can be attributed to the literary and pop-culture image of the perfect birth. When you read books that describe unmedicated vaginal birth as the most powerful and beautiful moment a woman can experience, and you read baby magazines where celebrities describe their births as miraculous and serene, it is easy to feel as though you opened the wrong door: instead of winning the blissful trip to Mommy Nirvana, you got handed the case of Turtle Wax.

"I felt cheated by my births," said Tricia, a stay-at-home mother of two in Clarks Summit, Pennsylvania. "I thought everything would go smoothly, and it didn't. I really wanted to go natural, but I had terrible back labor with my first delivery, so I got the epidural. And the second time, I felt rotten through the entire pregnancy and then had an emergency C-section six weeks early. I didn't get to enjoy the deliveries at all. I had watched many hours of *A Baby Story*, and I wanted that wonderful experience of having the baby put on my chest and falling instantly in love, but it didn't happen that way at all."

So the moms may be disappointed that it didn't work out perfectly this time, but they take their baby and go home. The next few weeks and months are a blur of getting to know that baby, getting used to their new life, and emerging from that sleep-deprived, hormone-addled new mommy daze. And once they are finally able to put their thoughts together and process the events of their baby's birth, an interesting dichotomy occurs. For one subset of these moms, the disappointment melts into acceptance. They look back at their birth experience as something that wasn't ideal but was necessary to bring their baby into the world. "Yes, it was disappointing that I didn't get to deliver naturally," said Jennie, who gave birth to her second child via C-section after laboring for twelve hours with no progress. "The whole process wasn't as nice as my first delivery. In fact, when they handed me the baby, I actually said, 'Hold on a minute, I have to vomit first,' so it wasn't exactly the perfect moment I was looking for. But I wasn't depressed at all afterward, and I don't have any regrets about it. We did what was best for the baby, and in the long run, it really doesn't matter. You feel the same about your child no matter how he came out."

The other subset of moms, however, has a much harder time with it. They come out of the post-delivery daze shellshocked and wondering what the hell happened. They find it difficult, if not impossible, to let it go. I've found that the biggest difference between these two groups was in how they perceived they were treated by their doctor or midwife. If a woman truly believes, like Jennie and Naomi did, that her doctor was with her all the way, that he or she was making decisions that were in the best interest of the mother and child, then it is far easier for her to accept the outcome of the delivery.

But if there is a moment of doubt, a moment when the mom looks back and concludes that she was manipulated into an intervention that was not entirely necessary, then that daze and disappointment can easily turn to anger. "After my C-section, I felt so angry. I felt like I'd been had," said Beth, who labored for some thirty hours at home before heading into the hospital, where she ultimately had a C-section. "For the next two years, I obsessively read everything that was out there, all the anti-C-section material. And I said, 'Oh my god, how did I think that I hadn't been walked down this path?' I had done all the research and picked an OB with a low C-section rate, but in the end, I truly believe *once a surgeon, always a surgeon.* I remember going to my childbirth-class reunion with the babies, and no one could believe that I ended up with a C-section. I couldn't believe it myself."

Lila from Dallas, who was induced a week early to fit her nurse's schedule and then had her daughter yanked out with forceps after a grueling labor, felt anger toward her doctor and the standard medical protocols he followed. But she also felt pissed off at herself for never thinking to question those standards. "I did not appreciate the way I was manhandled, but at the time I just chalked up my experience to bad luck," she said. "I can't put all the blame on the doctor, because it was my responsibility to educate myself, and if I had learned more about it, I would not have agreed to a lot of the things he did. But I put my blind faith in him, and at the end of the day, people act on their own best interest instead of yours."

While Lila and Beth both felt it was the impersonal, standardized hospital policies that led them to deeply unsatisfying birth experiences, I have also heard from mothers who were disillusioned by their midwives and their birth centers, which they had chosen because they believed they would give them the best chance for a gentle, safe birth. In the end, they felt that the midwives were unprepared to deal with anything but a picture-perfect delivery. "All through my pregnancy, the midwives told me I was the perfect candidate for the birth center," said Julia, a decorator and mother of three in New York. "I knew it would hurt, but maybe it would take five hours, there would be dim light and candles, and it would be great. Instead, I had back labor for five days, and I was in so much pain that I could barely speak or see. I couldn't move, I couldn't get in a bath or try any laboring positions. I literally crawled into a cab and went to the birth center. When I got there, I was dilated less than a centimeter, so they sent me home. I tried to tell them that something was wrong, but I couldn't speak, and my husband was in such shock that he couldn't do anything to advocate for me. My water finally broke in the cab on the way home, and we went back to the birth center. The midwives there kept saying, 'Come on, nothing's wrong, if you keep talking like this, you're going to have a C-section.' They made me feel like a spoiled brat, like I wasn't strong enough to do it. I was left alone in a room. When I finally went past the time limit, they put me in a cab again and sent me to the hospital."

Once at the hospital, the place she had so desperately hoped to avoid, Julia said she found the care and support that was missing at the birth center. "It was a full moon, and it seemed as if every woman in New York was giving birth that night, but as soon as the doctor saw me, he made up a bed for me and gave me an IV," she recalled. "I hadn't had anything to eat or drink in days, and I was so dehydrated that my labor had stopped. At the birth center, all they gave me was Gatorade, which I power-vomited all over the room. Two wonderful nurses stayed with me, one putting pressure on my back and the other stroking my face and telling me everything was going to be fine. I agreed to an epidural, and then I fell asleep for ten hours. When I woke up, I was ready to push. I pushed for about an hour, and my beautiful baby girl was born.

"The thing that makes me so mad," Julia continued, "is that in all my childbirth classes, I was told that an epidural was dangerous for me and my baby, and that it could only help with the pain but couldn't stop it, and that was a lie. I was so scared of the epidural, and as a result I had five days of excruciating labor. I felt such a backlash, like if I had been tougher and stronger, I could have done it. It took me a few years to realize that just wasn't true."

Julia told me of feeling for months as if she had personally failed, a feeling that was seconded by several of the women who had disappointing births, especially those who had hoped to go natural. (A study in the journal *Birth* found that one in four women who had undergone an emergency C-section blamed themselves at least in part for failing to deliver vaginally.)[2] It's no surprise that so many women feel that way when the concept of failure is built right into the language. The actual medical terminology for a labor that doesn't move along fast enough is *failure to progress*.

Deliver This!

For women who have so much control and success in other areas of their lives, that sense of failure can hit particularly hard, putting them off childbirth altogether. "I am a real type-A personality, and I did everything I could to have the perfect pregnancy and birth," said Helen, a finance executive in Providence, Rhode Island. "I exercised every day and only ate all-natural food. Everything was fine until my seventh month, when I started having contractions. I was put on bed rest for the remainder of my pregnancy, and it was miserable. I still planned on natural birth, but when I finally went into labor for real, the contractions came on so strong that it was unbearable. I tried walking and taking a shower and got into different positions, but I became paralyzed with pain. When I got to the hospital, I begged for an epidural, but the anesthesiologist was doing an emergency C-section and couldn't get to me in time, so I wound up doing natural birth after all. The whole experience was so unbelievably painful and unpleasant that it just soured me on the whole idea of childbirth."

Then there is the no-win game of second-guessing everything that happened along the way. Several women told me how they kept rewinding that day and playing it over and over again in their minds, trying to figure out what they could have done or said to make things turn out differently. "I wonder what would have happened if I had given birth in the wilderness or lived a century ago," said Alexandra, a New York lawyer who planned on natural labor in a hospital birth center but agreed to a C-section after forty-two hours of labor, including six hours of pushing without the baby crowning. "I think if I hadn't been so concerned about the hospital's time frame after my water breaking, I wouldn't have worked so hard to get my labor going that first night at home, and I would have slept more, which might have given me more energy to keep pushing. My midwife and the OB both told me that based on his size, they didn't think my son could have been born vaginally without harming him or me, but I find it hard to believe that nature would have allowed a child to grow beyond his mother's capacity to birth him. Maybe I'm naive—and I know that women die in childbirth— but I can't help but wonder what would have happened if I had had a full chance to birth him on my own."

Unfortunately, there is no magic replay pod that can take you back in time and give you a do-over on your baby's day of birth. You have to look forward. You have to find a way to deal with the lingering emotions of a disappointing birth so you can fully embrace the business of being a mom. And here's where the whole Mommy World culture can be your lifeline. Yes, there is plenty of judgment floating around about why you might have chosen that kind of birth plan to begin with, and, as ugly as it is, someone may whisper behind your back that you sealed your own fate by choosing a birth center or having an epidural or trusting your doctor, but there is also a tremendous amount of support to be found out there.

Many moms find it helpful to go on websites such as BabyCenter.com, where they can share their experiences with sympathetic listeners across the country. Others find that hiring a postpartum doula can be especially helpful, as well as discussing the birth with their doctor or midwife, or even, as one mom said, "calling that twenty-four-hour nursing hotline at the hospital just to talk things out in the middle of the night." But most of all, they find their solace in their friendships with other moms. "I had really bad feelings about myself," said Julia. "It wasn't intensely with me every moment, but it nagged at me for two or three years. I joined a support group, where I heard stories from women who had every kind of birth. Everyone said to me, 'You did nothing wrong, you did everything right.' And I needed to hear that from other women who had recently gone through it."

The most positive thing to be taken away from a disappointing birth experience (other than the baby, of course) is that it can really help you focus on what you want and how you can do it differently the next time. Of course, some moms decided—because of their age, their fertility, their difficulties with the previous birth, or simply their contentment with the size of their family—that they weren't going to go through it again. But the moms who did go on to have another baby did so with a new determination to make their follow-up experience more satisfying. They brainstormed about what they could do differently, and how it could be better. They switched to new doctors or midwives who they felt were more in sync with their goals. They educated themselves on interventions.

Lila, who felt manhandled by her doctor, chose to deliver

her second baby in a birth center with a midwife. Beth, who was devastated by an emergency C-section, delivered her two younger children at home (though VBAC at home is an extremely controversial choice and not all midwives will agree to attend them). Julia, who had the miserable birth-center experience, adored the doctor who delivered her child at the hospital and went back to him for her second and third babies. Sally, like the majority of emergency C-section moms, scheduled a repeat C-section for her next child and was relieved to be able to go into the hospital emotionally prepared for surgery. Three years after her negative experience, Helen is starting to entertain the idea of giving it another go, but she said she can also foresee a happy future raising just one lovely little girl.

Claudia, who "risked out" of her birth center and had to deliver in a hospital, was just as passionate about having an unassisted birth with her second baby, but on the second go-round she deliberately left open a small window to accommodate the idea that things might not go exactly according to plan. "When I had to check into the hospital last time, it was like a comedy of errors. I was asking the nurse where the maternity ward was, and she thought I was there to visit someone," Claudia recalls. "So this time, we're actually going to take the hospital tour. I also feel like I will know what to say. If they tell me I have to wear the hospital gown or I can't eat, I will just tell them to call my midwife." When she did give birth to her second child, though, Claudia got to deliver just as she had wished—in the birth center, with no interventions, with the midwives standing by, but basically leaving her alone. "My husband helped pull the shoulders through, but that was it," she said proudly. "I did this 99 percent on my own."

In the end, the two most helpful tools for moving on from a disappointing birth experience are the distance that time brings and the passion you feel for your baby. No matter what the circumstance of their delivery, every mom I spoke to said the disappointment, anger, and sadness get smaller and more insignificant every day. "I had to take the time to process it," said Alexandra. "There were some emotional bumps along the way, but it's something I've come to terms with. But you know what? In time, your priorities change. You have a baby who is healthy and happy, and you're alive to see it, which is much more important than the circumstances of the birth. And my son is just so awesome!"

## CHAPTER TWELVE

# The *DELIVER THIS!* PLAN *for* GIVING BIRTH YOUR WAY

As I wrapped up each interview for this book, after talking about inductions and doulas and annoying in-laws and judgmental friends, I made sure to save a moment at the end of each of our conversations to ask one final question: *What did it really, truly feel like the very first moment you held your baby?* I wanted to know if these moms had experienced that mythical, spontaneous, head-over-heels love. Or did they just stare at the baby and think, *Hmmm, interesting. I have a baby. So now what do I do?*

My motives were scientific, of course. I wanted to cut through that hazy fog of the "mommy bliss" myth that baby magazines, TV shows, books, and message boards perpetuate on a daily basis—that guilt-inducing misconception that love always happens the same way: As soon as you lock eyes with your child, you are changed forever and your bond is instant and infallible. Jeez, don't we have enough pressure on us already? With these great expectations of transcendence, how can we feel anything but disappointed if the reality does not match up to the hype?

But the truth is, I needed to know the answer for myself, too.

A confession: I adore my daughters. I think they are two of the funniest, most adorable creatures who ever walked the face of the earth. But that love did not emerge fully formed along with the afterbirth. It has grown day by day, created from all those quotidian moments together: falling asleep on the couch with the baby on my chest, endless readings of *Go, Dog. Go!*, our ritual Tuesday night *American Idol* pajama party, the squeaky but earnest sound of my three-year-old singing "You Are My Sunshine." And this makes sense. When my babies were born, I felt a physical connection to them (after all, they had been kicking, elbowing, and hiccuping inside of me for months), but I had not gotten to know them yet as anything other than an extension of myself. The more I held them, studied them, got to know their personalities and feel the powerful presence of their love for me, the deeper I fell for them. And you know what? I never would have thought it should be any other way.

But then when I open up a baby magazine and read a profile of model/mom Emme, who says, "The bond you instantly share with your child is the most beautiful thing in the world,"[1] or when I turn on an episode of *A Baby Story*— really, pick an episode, any one—and Debbie or Beth or Linda rocks her baby, looks into the camera and says, "I was shocked at how much love I immediately felt for little Cate-lyn/Jasmine/Dylan," I feel like I must have been the most coldhearted new mom in New York.

When Bellamy was first handed to me, wearing nothing but a hospital blanket and a teeny purple cap, I felt many things—exhaustion, hunger, gratitude, peace, curiosity—but I can't honestly say I felt *Love* with a capital L. I didn't feel that Vulcan mind meld Emme describes. In fact, if you had to narrow my reaction down to a single, overwhelming emotion, it was a tidal wave of relief that everything had ended well. Since I had been having recurring dreams throughout my pregnancy of giving birth to either a cyclops or a small gray kitten, I was almost irrationally relieved that Bellamy was recognizable as a human child. I was also relieved that my seemingly endless labor was over, and that the searing pain I had felt only twelve hours earlier was receding as a distant memory. I stared at my new daughter, trying to see my face in hers. She seemed so fragile to me: She had impossibly tiny hands, and she was no longer in the protective fortress of my belly. In my first act as an overprotective new mother, I memorized the circular pattern of white pimples on her nose just in case the babies got switched around in the nursery.

But, alas, no paroxysms of maternal adoration. So I have to think, *Did I miss something that all other moms experience?* Or is this myth of instant love something one mischievous mom made up, and in this hyped-up mommy culture, new mothers have been trying to live up to it ever since?

When a mother does attempt to pierce the veil of idealized baby love and speak an uncomfortable truth, she gets vilified. Just look at the reaction that greeted author Ayelet Waldman when she wrote in a *New York Times* essay that she felt more passion for her husband than for her four children.[2] While there were many women who said, "Thank god someone is saying what I feel," plenty of others dismissed her as a cold-hearted bitch who valued hot sex over motherhood.

That same dichotomy of acknowledging maternal ambivalence, yet being shocked that someone dares to admit it, can be found in our attitudes about the first moment of holding our children. In public—especially on TV and in magazines—new moms recite those lines that every "good mother" is supposed to feel.

But in private, I found that not everyone's experience fit quite so neatly into that script.

"I was squatting down, and then all of a sudden I saw this baby being thrown at me, and he was all wet and slimy. I was thinking, *What is this thing?* He looked so strange, like a little alien, with smushed features," said a mom who delivered in a hospital birth center. "It was not love at first sight at all. I was just happy he was healthy." Other moms told me they were afraid to hold the baby, or they were fine with their partner holding him first, because frankly, all they wanted to do was rest. Or they stared at the baby and saw a stranger. But every mother said that when she really got to know her baby, after a few days or weeks or months, she did eventually fall in love.

So listen up all you moms who didn't feel like bursting into a Whitney Houston ballad the moment your baby entered the world: It's safe to come out now.

While I found it comforting to know that plenty of other moms with all kinds of birth stories—natural and medicated, C-section and vaginal—admitted that their love took a little time to grow, I also have come to believe that the moms who swore to me that they did have that "special moment," that spontaneous passion, were speaking the truth about their own experiences.

One mother I interviewed who had had a C-section recalled, "A friend of mine told me, 'You cannot fathom the intensity of love you will feel for this child. It is irrational and surreal.' Well, it wasn't quite *that* dramatic, but when I held her, I definitely did feel an overpowering love for her. I couldn't stop touching her and couldn't take my eyes off her." Moms who had natural births in particular talked about "that awesome moment" of seeing or touching their babies for the first time. It is sometimes difficult to separate the joy about the labor from the child itself, since most of these moms spoke of a general euphoria that encompassed the entire experience. Descriptions of the exhilaration included, "Oh, we *so* had that moment. I was feeling great, we were holding the baby together, and everything was fine," and, "I was absolutely pumped as soon as I felt her come out." Their zeal was about their relationships with their babies, but it was also about their relationship with their bodies. These issues seemed blissfully interconnected, which is one of the philosophies behind natural birth.

So the big question for me was, does our birth choice dictate whether we will experience that instant love? Did giving birth in a hospital with an epidural rob me of my special moment? Did another mother's choice to have an elective C-section make her experience any less poignant than that of a mother who opted for giving birth in a tub at a birth center? It is undeniable that the moms who put more thought, effort, and preparation into their babies' births and who look at it as a holistic, life-defining moment are more likely to experience some sort of postnatal euphoria. (Also, it must be noted, they may be more likely to feel anger and failure if their plan doesn't work out.) These moms have more invested in the experience to begin with, and the entire labor process is one huge personal journey for them, culminating in the emotionally powerful moment of birth. For moms who go against the mainstream and have babies at home or in birth centers, there is the added victory of giving birth on their own terms. All those incredibly positive feelings are naturally going to spill over into their emotions upon holding their newborn babies.

But there's more to it than that. Having a baby naturally, or vaginally, or outside of a hospital does not guarantee insta-love (one of the most ardent natural-birth advocates I interviewed said she did not feel that immediate bond until she had her third child), just as having drugs or a C-section does not preclude it. In fact, several of the C-section moms reported that even though they had to wait a little longer than they had hoped to have some one-on-one time, they did feel a deep emotional bond as soon as the baby was in their arms. Many of them experienced a mirror image of what the natural-birth moms felt: After having gone through what is, in many cases, an emotionally *un*satisfying birth experience—one that goes against their plans and desires and is punctuated by the fear that the baby's life is in danger—that moment when a healthy and squawking baby is finally lifted out of their abdomen provides an enormous emotional catharsis, creating an overwhelming surge of love for the baby. The bumpy road to the joy and love may be very different, but the knockout punch it brings can be just as powerful.

So yes, the circumstances of the birth certainly do play a part in your emotional reaction to it, but if we back up and examine the influences and life experiences that *lead* you to that birth center or hospital or elective C-section in the first place, it is clear that those factors are also going to help determine your emotional response upon being presented with your child. In addition to your feelings about your body, your politics, and your relationship with your partner, your history with babies in general and this baby in particular will come into play: the length of time and amount of energy or intervention it took to conceive this baby; your history of pregnancies and miscarriages; whether this is your first or fifth child; whether you feel financially and emotionally ready to be a parent; and how deeply the idea of motherhood is intertwined with your image of yourself.

I, for one, never felt the baby jones that so many other women talk about—the palpable ache inside when walking past the babyGap at the mall or playing Candyland with a friend's three-year-old. In fact, until my girls were born, I had never held a baby for more than a few minutes at a time. I had no younger siblings, no nieces or nephews; I never played with Barbies or baby dolls, and I had never changed a diaper. (My husband, on the other hand, who had spent many afternoons as a teenager baby-sitting for his younger half-sister, had a much stronger, instant attachment to our kids.)

A woman who already knows what it is like to adore a baby is going to experience a double charge of, "Wow, it's a baby, and wow, it's *mine!*" Personality plays a big part in this, too. Some people are just more emotionally open than others, and some bond more easily with new people, no matter their size. "I had a tough time attaching to my baby right away," admitted a mom who gave birth in a hospital. "I didn't feel that love for a month or so. But that's just me—I always warm up to people more slowly."

So, after a little self-analysis, I have come to the conclusion that just as my life experiences and preferences would not have made natural birth an appropriate choice for me, those same forces molded me into one of those moms who took a little time to fall deep into the baby-love ocean. And I am completely at peace with that. I did what was right for me, and I felt the emotions that were only natural for me at the time. And it was all part of creating the family that I am so unabashedly in love with.

Ultimately, this journey of figuring out who I am and what I value has only increased the admiration I feel for the women who choose a vastly different childbirth path than mine. Especially knowing how difficult it is in to go against the grain and choose anything but a standard hospital birth, I respect each mother for the integrity of knowing who she is and for having the courage to fight for what is best for her. When I talk to women who have had great home births or birth-center births or natural births, I am excited for them. I love hearing their stories of perseverance and triumph in the same way I love watching a really inspiring sports movie. I know it was not the right choice for me, but I can understand how it was absolutely the best choice for them.

But in order for us to stop the judgment and the eye-rolling, to silence that sense of disapproval that injects so much negative energy into what should be a supportive community of new moms, we all need to acknowledge that what was an amazing experience for one woman might simply be painful and tedious for another. What seems safe and comfortable for one might only be constrictive and dehumanizing to another. An experience can only be transcendent if it speaks to the values you have developed over a lifetime. I know that the type of birth that felt so right for me would have been absolutely intolerable for someone else.

Which is why we are so lucky we have the gift of choice.

Now, I know this is not a utopian society where we have completely unfettered access to any type of birth we desire. It sucks that health insurance companies often limit our options of who can assist in our birth and where we can go to labor, and it sucks that the fear of malpractice lawsuits forces some doctors to consider things other than the mother's wishes. It also bites that VBACs are rarely considered a legitimate option. But there are also many great things about the state of childbirth today. Unlike during previous decades, when there was really only one way to do things, when male doctors wielded an unchallenged paternal authority over their female patients, now we have more choices than ever. Though independent birth centers do not exist everywhere, new ones open up every year. More and more hospitals are creating natural-birth rooms as an alternative to the standard labor and delivery ward. Midwives in every state are available to assist home births. Epidurals and surgical techniques are being improved every day. And thanks to the global community of the Internet, you can find up-to-date information about every type of birth, instant connections to midwives and doulas, and mom-to-mom support no matter where you live, how isolated you feel, or how disapproving your friends and family may be.

The secret behind knowing which birth option is "best" is knowing which birth option is best *for you*. Yes, fervent believers in every corner will argue that there is a single superior method of delivering a baby. They will say that a home birth cannot be as safe as a hospital birth (or vice versa), or that a C-section cannot be as safe as a vaginal birth (or vice versa). There may be slight statistical differences in some areas, but the truth is that healthy, lovely, smart children have been born at home, in birth centers, after emergency C-sections, and with epidurals. In plowing through the research, it became clear to me that the most important ingredients in a successful, healthy birth are good prenatal care, the supervision of a qualified and compassionate doctor or midwife, and a good backup plan in case there are complications. I have yet to find any strong science out there that proves that the type of birth you choose will make any difference at all in terms of what kind of baby you produce.

After all is said and done, what matters the most when it comes to a low-risk pregnancy is the mother's ability to labor and deliver in the place where she feels safest and most in control (exactly what it is she wants to control is the big variable, of course). It is all about *you*. It is about which experience will put you in the best possible frame of mind to start being a mother. Some women get to this place by taking charge, trusting their body to do what it needs to do, going through the hard work of natural labor, and reaping the emotional rewards from succeeding at it. Others feel they are best launched into the role of mom after being relaxed, anesthetized, and surrounded by the most high-tech environment just in case something goes wrong. You have to go into your birth experience convinced that your personal needs and concerns will be respected. You have to do what you feel in your heart is best for your baby.

So, I know it's a lot to think about. I also know that there are a million other issues fighting for a pregnant woman's

time and attention (just dealing with the constant need for
new, larger sizes of underwear can drive you crazy). It's very
tempting to put the whole issue of childbirth on the back
burner and figure you'll deal with it when the time comes.
But we can learn so much about ourselves and that community of mothers we're joining by facing the facts and choices
of childbirth head-on. I didn't think about it all, and though
I had two perfectly satisfying births, I readily admit that
there are things that could have played out better. Had I
pushed aside my fear and all my preconceived notions about
birth and read up on it and listened to what other moms
were trying to tell me, I would have done some things very
differently. Having now heard from so many moms about
the amazingly soothing powers of water, I would have tried
taking a hot bath or shower to see if that could have helped
me get through the first throes of pain. I definitely, *definitely*
would have said no to the Stadol. It did not do anything
for my pain. Instead it gave me those weird unicorn hal-
lucinations, and, as I learned later, Stadol is delivered in
a much higher dose than the drugs in an epidural, which
means more of it might have reached the baby.[3] Also, now
that I have seen the latest studies on early-labor epidurals, I
would have talked to my doctor about the possibility of getting one before I hit the magic four-centimeter mark. Most
importantly, I would have prepared myself for the possibility of my labor going longer than twenty-four hours, and
I would have known how to argue if my doctor had really
pushed for a C-section. And if it had come down to it and

I did need a surgical birth, I would have gone in knowing what to expect.

My primary goal in writing this book was to help women understand the benefits of different birth options and help them choose the one that makes the most sense for their personality, values, and circumstances. And after talking to scores of women who have given birth every which way, asking them what they loved, what they hated, what worked best for them, and how they would do it differently, I have come up with the Mom-knows-best, ten-point *Deliver This!* plan for designing the most satisfying—and, yes, maybe even ecstatic—birth possible:

**1. Take the time to know yourself.** You can't change who you are to mold yourself to someone else's idea of what the best or safest birth plan is, so take the time to think about what makes you tick and what you really want. Ask yourself first: If you had completely free will, without considering insurance, your family's opinion, or your doctor's preferences, how would you want to bring your baby into the world? What are your hopes and fears about childbirth? How strongly do you believe in the mind-body connection? Do you value comfort over endurance? Do you get satisfaction from a hard physical workout, or just pain? Do doctors and hospitals make you think of safety and healing, or danger and illness? Are you okay with following rules you didn't write yourself? What are your political and social views about childbirth? Do you feel most empowered in a partnership, or do you want someone who will take charge of the situation? Are there any health factors that cause you to believe this birth might not go smoothly?

Hopefully, after reading the previous chapters, one of the birth options made you sit up and say, "Yes! That makes total sense! Those moms sound just like me!" Meanwhile, I'm sure that some other chapters made you squirm and think, *Yikes, I would never do that in a million years.* Your gut reaction will tell you a lot about which choice will ultimately be right for you, but don't stop there.

**2. Take a peek at the other side.** This may seem counterintuitive, but it's an important step in understanding the issues and reinforcing your belief that you have made the right choice. If you are leaning toward natural birth, go ahead and immerse yourself in *Birthing from Within* and *The Bradley Method*, but also take some time to read materials that argue for the *positive* side of medicated birth. If you are absolutely set on a hospital birth, read up on birth centers and home births. If you skipped right over those chapters in this book, go back and give them a quick look. You might discover that your choice does not have to be all-or-nothing: Elements of one birth option can be incorporated into a somewhat different one, and understanding the entire spectrum of options will be crucial if your plans have to change at the last minute. And, just as important, when you come across another mom—perhaps one of those cousins you see twice a year or a neighbor you meet in the local sandbox—and she tells you she gave birth an entirely different way than you did, you can get past the puzzlement and move on to understanding.

**3. Let go of the fear.** I allowed my fear of pain to keep me from really looking hard at all the options. And while there is no way anyone can convince me that what I felt in my back and stomach on those two July days was not a real, overwhelming physical sensation, I do acknowledge that the fear may have made it even worse. But here's the thing: While the pain is real, so are the many, many different options for alleviating it. So instead of fixating on how bad you expect the pain to feel, focus on how you can handle it, whether it is through Hypnobirth, water birth, relaxation mantras, or an epidural.

**4. Get the scoop by talking to real women.** Baby reality shows and magazine features are fun and addictive, but they do not give you the whole story. Remember that those subjects are carefully chosen, and their stories are highly edited to produce a desired emotional reaction or push a specific agenda. To get the raw, unfiltered story, filled with the nitty-gritty details that all those shows leave out, talk to women who have been through the kind of birth you desire. If you don't know anyone personally who has been there, ask your midwife, doctor, birth center, or doula to hook you up with other women who can give you an honest narrative of what really goes down.

**5. Choose your doctor or midwife as carefully as you chose your spouse.** Seriously. The single most important factor in creating a birth experience in which you feel your wishes and needs are truly being met is finding a doctor or midwife whom you absolutely trust. Don't worry about being polite. You can ditch your longtime doctor if you have doubts about her childbirth policies or about whether she is completely in sync with you. You can even switch mid-pregnancy, though ideally you should get it all sorted out by the second trimester so you can build a relationship with your new doctor or midwife before the big day. Interview as many people as you can until you feel completely comfortable. And then, if you can, interview his or her partners, since there's a good chance your baby will be delivered by someone other than the person you chose. You know that person on every hospital tour or birth-center information session who asks eight million annoying questions? That should be you.

**6. Understand the rules.** Think about every procedure or standard intervention that could possibly crop up in the course of your labor, and talk to your doctor or midwife about any concerns you might have about them. At what point would you need to be transferred to a regular hospital delivery room? How early will your doctor allow you to get the epidural? Does the hospital require continual fetal monitoring, or will you be able to get up and walk around if you wish? What kind of natural inductions will you be allowed to try before Pitocin gets involved? How often does your doctor perform episiotomies, and will he give you a say in the matter? How strict is the twenty-four-hour-labor rule? If your gut feeling is to leave those choices up to your doctor, then fine. But if you have any issues, bring them up now, and if you have any concern at all that your doctor might not remember what he promised you in the consultation, write down a list of your preferences and make sure your partner or doula brings a copy to the delivery room.

**7. Don't listen to anyone else.** If you even hint at the fact that you are considering an alternative birth plan, particularly a home birth or an elective C-section, people will crawl out of the woodwork to tell you you're crazy and will try to talk you out of it. So it's best not to discuss it with any friends, family, or coworkers until your plans have been made and you are absolutely certain of your decision. Even then, you may want to keep things vague so as not to let other people's opinions muddle your own thinking and make you second-guess your choice. Choose one or two friends to confide in who you know will be supportive and open-minded. And don't feel the need to be completely honest with every stranger who stops you on the street, pats your belly, and asks where you're delivering. No matter what they may think, it's just none of their damn business.

**8. Prepare for your baby's birth like it's a shuttle launch.** If you are planning anything other than a scheduled C-section, sign up for classes that will help you prepare physically and mentally for the birth and will also introduce you to a community of pregnant women with the same mind-set. (Don't count on the standard hospital childbirth class to teach you much more than the stages of labor and which floor the maternity ward is on.) And make sure your partner does the work, too, by figuring out how he or she can best assist you in the labor room and what to say if you can't speak for yourself. If you need more support, enlist a friend who has been through childbirth herself, or hire a doula.

**9. Keep an open mind.** Remember that in the end, you cannot have complete control over your baby's birth. Even the most meticulous plans can get screwed up. Sit down, close your eyes, and picture a scenario where your labor stalls, you get transferred to a hospital, or you have to have a C-section, and imagine what you will say and how you will cope with it. And no matter what your feelings about C-sections are, make sure you read at least one chapter of one book describing what is involved in a surgical birth. It may be information that you never need to use, but if you do wind up in the operating room, at least you will know what to expect.

**10. Let it go.** Hopefully, after following the previous nine steps, you will be able to achieve the birth experience you want. And in that case, once it's over, go ahead and exult in the joy of your new baby. If things do not go exactly as you planned, you need to know that it is not your fault. You have not failed if you need a C-section. You have not failed if you ask for drugs. You have not failed if you don't have that emotional explosion of instant baby-love. In the end, childbirth is just the kickoff to the great new adventure that lies ahead. So get the support you need, do what you have to do to take care of your baby, and look forward to all those awesome, hilarious, deeply moving, and sometimes magical moments of motherhood that await you in the future.

# ACKNOWLEDGMENTS

Over the past year, I have talked to women everywhere about their birth choices—on the phone, over coffee, via email, sitting on the crosstown bus. This book would not have been possible without their incredible generosity and openness, and I thank each and every one for their time and their stories.

Also, for their invaluable insight, I extend my gratitude to Deanne Williams and Tim Clarke at the American College of Nurse-Midwives; Kate Bauer at the American Association of Birth Centers; Cherie Boettcher, CNM; Joan Bryson, CNM; Andrea Christenson, CNM; Cathy Parisi, CNM; Susan Stapleton, CNM; Jacques Moritz, MD; Laurel Walter, MD; Mark Rosing, MD; Rachel Masch, MD; Gilbert Grant, MD; and the library staff at the Museum of Television and Radio.

Anyone who has tried to write a book while raising two small children knows it would be an impossible task without trusted and loving babysitters, so my everlasting thanks go to Gloria and Mel Cohen, Charlotte Ehrman, Lindsey Freedman, and Julie Rothman.

For support and enthusiasm above and beyond the call of duty, and for playdates and lunch dates that kept me sane, thanks to Sharon Boone, Catherine Boursier, Elise Caccappolo, Sarah Chumsky, Michael Cohen, Jeanne Dupont, Lex Fink, Ellen Hwang, Sharon Israel, Melissa Morgenlander, Hope Newman, Julia Parker, Randi Pellett, Jennifer Ritter, Theresa Schultz, Lisa Smith, Josh Tager, Julie Turaj, Kathleen Reynolds, and Nanette Varian. Extra-special shout-outs go to Ellie Wertheim, for being the first friend to read these pages and offer encouragement, and Lauren Wittels, for expertly and selflessly transcribing hours of tapes.

In a miracle of modern conception, *Deliver This!* had more than one woman responsible for its birth. I have the world's most patient and dedicated agent in Jennie Dunham, who was so incredibly supportive of this project that she gave birth to her second child just as I was finishing up. I also had the world's most enthusiastic and caring editor in Brooke Warner, who helped me figure out how all these random thoughts about childbirth would make an actual book.

And finally, none of this would have happened without the support of my wonderful husband, Jeremy Richardson, who held my hand through the labor pains of two daughters and one book.

# RESOURCE GUIDE

## Websites

### Choices in Childbirth
www.choicesinchildbirth.com
(248) 835-5808
Information on choosing natural childbirth in a variety
of settings

### Holistic Moms Network
www.holisticmoms.org
(877) HOL-MOMS
Support and information on natural childbirth and
alternative parenting

## Doulas of North America

www.dona.org

(888) 788-DONA

Referrals to certified doulas for childbirth and postpartum care

## American College of Nurse-Midwives

www.mymidwife.org

(240) 485-1800

Information on midwifery care and referrals to Certified Nurse-Midwives and Certified Midwives

## Midwives Alliance of North America

www.mana.org

(888) 923-MANA

Information and referrals to all categories of midwives, including direct-entry

## Citizens for Midwifery

www.cfmidwifery.org

(888) CfM-4880

Education and resources to promote the midwifery model of care

## North American Registry of Midwives

http://narm.org

Information and certification for Certified Professional Midwives

**American Association of Birth Centers**
www.birthcenters.org
(215) 234-8068
State-by-state directory of AABC-certified independent
childbirth centers

**Association of Labor Assistants and Childbirth Educators**
www.alace.org
(617) 441-2500
Information on becoming a childbirth assistant/educator,
and some state-by-state listings of labor coaches

**Birthpartners.com**
www.birthpartners.com
(970) 389-311
Lists of midwives, doulas, and other natural-childbirth
practitioners

**Childbirth Connection**
www.childbirthconnection.org
(212) 777-5000
Information on woman-centered childbirth

**International Cesarean Awareness Network**
www.ican-online.org
(800) 686-ICAN
Information on lowering the rate of C-sections, support for
C-section recovery, and promotion of VBACs

**American College of Obstetricians and Gynecologists**
www.acog.org
(202) 638-5577
Extensive listings of OB/GYNs, plus news about
women's health

**National Women's Health Information Center**
www.4women.gov
(800) 994-9662
General information and articles on pregnancy, childbirth,
and breastfeeding

## Natural-Childbirth Classes

**Bradley Method**
American Academy of Husband-Coached Childbirth
www.bradleybirth.com
(818) 788-6662

**Lamaze International**
www.lamaze.org
(800) 368-4404

**International Childbirth Education Association**
www.icea.org
(952) 854-8660

**Birthing from Within**
www.birthingfromwithin.com
(505) 254-4884

**BirthWorks**
www.birthworks.com
(888) TO-BIRTH

**HypnoBirthing**
www.hypnobirthing.com
(603) 798-3286

**Waterbirth International**
www.waterbirth.org
(800) 641-2229

## Websites for Moms

**Baby Center**
www.babycenter.com
Articles on every aspect of pregnancy and parenting,
plus an active on-line community of moms from all
across the country

**Urban Baby**
www.UrbanBaby.com
A space for moms to trade tips and uncensored opinions
on everything from birth choices to preschools to
sexual politics

**iVillage**

www.ivillage.com

A place to join an "expecting club" and chat with moms across the country who are due the same month as you

**Literary Mama**

www.literarymama.com

An online literary magazine with thought-provoking fiction, poetry, and essays by and about modern moms

# Books

### Natural Birth

Michel Odent and Grantley Dick-Read. *Childbirth Without Fear: The Principles and Practices of Natural Childbirth* (London: Pinter & Martin, Ltd., 2005).

Henci Goer and Rhonda Wheeler. *The Thinking Woman's Guide to a Better Birth* (New York: Perigee Books, 1999).

Ina May Gaskin. *Ina May's Guide to Childbirth* (New York: Bantam, 2003).

Pam England and Rob Horowitz. *Birthing from Within: An Extra-Ordinary Guide to Childbirth Preparation* (Albuquerque, NM: Partera Press, 1998).

Susan McCutcheon-Rosegg, Erick Ingraham, and Robert A. Bradley. *Natural Childbirth the Bradley Way* (New York: Plume, 1996).

Janet Balaskas. *Active Birth: The New Approach to Giving Birth Naturally* (Boston: Harvard Common Press, 1992).

## Medicated Birth

Gilbert J. Grant. *Enjoy Your Labor: A New Approach to Pain Relief for Childbirth* (White Plains, NY: Russell Hastings Press, 2005).

William Camann and Kathryn Alexander. *Easy Labor: Every Woman's Guide to Choosing Less Pain and More Joy During Childbirth* (New York: Ballantine Books, 2006).

# NOTES

## Chapter 1

1. Centers for Disease Control's National Center for Health Statistics, National Vital Statistics Report 54, no. 2, 2003.

2. Ibid.

## Chapter 2

1. Carla H. Hay, "Childbirth in America: A Historical Perspective," in *Who's Having This Baby? Perspectives on Birthing* (Lansing MI: Michigan State University Press, 2002).

2. Sandra Howell-White, *Birth Alternatives: How Women Select Childbirth Care (Contributions in Sociology)* (Westport, CT: Greenwood Press, 1999).

3. Edward Shorter, *A History of Women's Bodies* (New York: Basic Books, 1982), 139.

4. Carla H. Hay, "Childbirth in America: A Historical Perspective."

5. J. B. DeLee, "The Prophylactic Forceps Operations," *American Journal of Obstetrics ans Gynecology* 1 (October 1920): 24–44.

6. Carla H. Hay, "Childbirth in America: A Historical Perspective."

7. Edward Shorter, *A History of Women's Bodies.*

8. Edward Shorter, *A History of Women's Bodies,* 146.

9. Centers for Disease Control, "Achievements in Public Health, 1900–1999: Healthier Mothers and Babies," *MMWR Weekly* 48, no. 38 (October 1999): 849-58.

10. National Center for Health Statistics, Death: Final Data, 2003.

11. Maternal mortality estimates developed by WHO, UNICEF and

UNFPA, 2000.

12. Edward Shorter, *A History of Women's Bodies.*

13. Centers for Disease Control's National Center for Health Statistics, National Vital Statistics Report 54, no. 2, 2003.

14. Sandra Howell-White, *Birth Alternatives: How Women Select Childbirth Care.*

## Chapter 3

1. K. C. Johnson and B. A. Daviss, "Outcomes of Planned Home Births with Certified Professional Midwives: Large Prospective Study in North America," *British Medical Journal* 330 (June 2005): 1416.

2. *Guidelines of Perinatal Care,* 5th ed. (Elk Grove Village, IL: American Academy of Pediatrics and The American College of Obstetricians and Gynecologists, 2002), 25.

3. Jenny W. Y. Pang et al., "Outcomes of Planned Home Births in Washington State: 1989—1996," *Obstetrics & Gynecology* 100, no. 2 (August 2002): 253–59.

4. H. Tyson, "Outcomes of 1,001 Midwife-Attended Home Births in Toronto, 1983-1988," *Birth* 18, no. 1 (March 1991): 14–19.

5. R. E. Anderson and D. A. Anderson, "The Cost-Effectiveness of Home Birth," *Journal of Nurse-Midwifery* 44, no. 1 (January–February 1999): 30–35.

6. Centers for Disease Control's National Center for Health Statistics, National Vital Statistics Report 54, no. 2, 2003.

7. T. A. Wiegers et al., "Maternity Care in the Netherlands: The Changing Home Birth Rate," *Birth* 25, no. 3 (September 1998): 190–97.

8. Jenny W. Y. Pang et al., "Outcomes of Planned Home Births in Washington State: 1989–1996."

9. Centers for Disease Control's National Center for Health Statistics, National Vital Statistics Report 54, no. 2, 2003.

## Chapter 4

1. New York State Department of Health, Vital Statistics, 2003.

2. From the American Association of Birth Centers's member roster.

3. Centers for Disease Control's National Center for Health Statistics, National Vital Statistics Report 54, no.2, 2003.

4. E. Lieberman et al., "Results of the National Study of Vaginal Birth After Cesarean in Birth Centers," *Obstetrics & Gynecology* 104, no. 5 (November 2004): 933–42.

5. American College of Obstetricians and Gynecologists, "Researchers Advise Against Attempting VBACs in Birth Centers," press release, October 29, 2004.

6. J. P. Rooks, N. L. Weatherby et al., "Outcomes of Care in Birth Centers: The National Birth Center Study," *New England Journal of Medicine* 321, no. 26 (December 28, 1989): 1804–11.

7. A. Theoni et al., "Review of 1,600 water births. Does Water Birth Increase The Risk Of Neonatal Infection?" *Journal of Maternal–Fetal & Neonatal Medicine* 17, no. 5 (May 2005): 357–61.

## Chapter 5

1. American College of Nurse-Midwives, www.mymidwife.org.

2. Centers for Disease Control's National Center for Health Statistics, National Vital Statistics Report 54, no. 2, 2003.

3. Centers for Disease Control, "Live Births by Place of Delivery and Attendant, According to Race and Hispanic Origin: United States, Selected Years, 1975–95."

4. American College of Nurse-Midwives, "A Comparison of Certified Nurse-Midwives/Certified Midwives and Certified Professional Midwives."

5. American College of Nurse-Midwives, "What Is a Midwife?"

6. Midwives Alliance of North America, "Direct-Entry Midwifery—State-by-State Legal Status, April, 2006." www.mana.org.

7. North American Registry of Midwives, mission statement.

8. K. C. Johnson and B. A. Daviss, "Outcomes of Planned Home Births with Certified Professional Midwives: Large Prospective Study in North America," *British Medical Journal* 330 (June 2005): 1416.

9. Center for Disease Control's National Center for Health Statistics, National Vital Statistics Report 54, no. 2, 2003.

10. Courtesy Tim Clarke, American College of Nurse-Midwives.

11. Suzanne Arms, *Immaculate Deception: A New Look at Women and Childbirth in America.*

12. Edward Shorter, *A History of Women's Bodies.*

13. Carla H. Hay, "Childbirth in America: A Historical Perspective."

14. American College of Nurse-Midwives, "A Brief History of Nurse-Midwifery in the U.S."

15. K. D. Scott et al., "A Comparison of Intermittent and Continuous Support During Labor: A Meta-Analysis," *American Journal of Obstetrics & Gynecology* 180, no. 5 (May 1999): 1054–59.

16. Doulas of North America, Birth Doula Certification.

## Chapter 6

1. A. M. Cyna, G. L. McAuliffe, and M. I. Andrew, "Hypnosis For Pain Relief in Labour and Childbirth: A Systematic Review," *British Journal of Anaesthesia* 93, no. 4 (October 2004): 505–11.

2. Joanne Dozer and Shannon Baruth, "Epidural Epidemic-Drugs in Labor: Are They Really Necessary . . . or Even Safe?" *Mothering,* no. 95 (July/August 1999).

3. J. Zhang et al., "Does Epidural Analgesia Prolong Labor and Increase Risk of Cesarean Delivery? A Natural Experiment," *American Journal of Obstetrics & Gynecology* 185, no. 1 (July 2001): 128–34.

4. R. D. Vincent and D. H. Chestnut, "Epidural Analgesia During Labor," *American Family Physician* 58, no. 8 (November 1998): 1785–92.

## Chapter 7

1. R. D. Vincent and D. H. Chestnut, "Epidural Analgesia During Labor," *American Family Physician* 58, no. 8 (November 1998): 1785–92.

2. C. A. Wong et al., "The Risk of Cesarean Delivery with Neuraxial Analgesia Given Early Versus Late in Labor," *New England Journal of Medicine* 352, no. 7 (February 17, 2005): 655—65.

3. G. Ohel, "Early Versus Late Initiation if Epidural Analgesia in Labor: Does It Increase the Risk of Cesarean Section? A Randomized Trial,"

*American Journal of Obstetrics & Gynecology* 194, no. 3 (March 2006): 600–05.

4. J. Zhang et al., "Does Epidural Analgesia Prolong Labor and Increase Risk of Cesarean Delivery? A Natural Experiment," *American Journal of Obstetrics & Gynecology* 185, no. 1 (July 2001): 128–34.

5. Gilbert J. Grant, MD, *Enjoy Your Labor: A New Approach to Pain Relief for Childbirth* (White Plains, NY: Russell Hastings Press, 2005), 63.

6. J. Schaffir, "Sexual Intercourse at Term and Onset of Labor," *Obstetrics & Gynecology* 107, no. 6 (June 2006): 1310–14.

7. Gilbert J. Grant, *Enjoy Your Labor: A New Approach to Pain Relief for Childbirth*.

8. Ibid.

9. American College of Obstetricians and Gynecologists, "Rate of Episiotomy Plummets Over Past Two Decades," press release, February 2002.

10. J. Zhang et al., "U.S. National Trends in Labor Induction, 1989–1998," *Obstetrical & Gynecological Survey* 57, no. 8, (August 2002): 498–99.

11. Centers for Disease Control's National Center for Health Statistics, National Vital Statistics Report 54, no. 2, 2003.

12. Centers for Disease Control's National Center for Health Statistics, National Vital Statistics Report 52, no. 10, 2002.

## Chapter 9

1. Edward Shorter, *A History of Women's Bodies*.

2. Centers for Disease Control's National Center for Health Statistics, Preliminary Birth Data: Maternal and Infant Health, 2004.

3. Jane Eliot Sewell, *Cesarean Section: A Brief History* (Washington, D.C.: American College of Obstetricians and Gynecologists and National Library of Medicine, 1993).

4. Edward Shorter, *A History of Women's Bodies*.

5. Bulletin of the World Health Organization 79, no. 12, 2001.

6. The Department of Health and Human Services, "Healthy People" 2010, January 2000.

7. American Pregnancy Association, Breech Birth fact sheet.

8. The Mayo Clinic, "Twin Pregnancy: What Multiples Mean for Mom." www.mayoclinic.com.

9. American College of Obstetricians and Gynecologists, *Vaginal Birth After Previous Cesarean Delivery Practice Guidelines,* Practice Bulletin, no. 54, July 2004.

10. M. B. Landon et al., "Maternal and Perinatal Outcomes Associated with a Trial of Labor after Prior Cesarean Delivery," *New England Journal of Medicine* 351, no. 25 (December 16, 2004): 2581–89.

11. M. Lydon-Rochelle et al., "Risk of Uterine Rupture During Labor Among Women with a Prior Cesarean Delivery," *New England Journal of Medicine* 345, no. 1 (July 5, 2001): 3–8.

12. K. S. Toppenberg, "Uterine Rupture: What Family Physicians Need to Know," *American Family Physician* 66, no. 5 (September 1, 2002): 823–8.

13. International Cesarean Awareness Network, "Coerced Cesarean Surgeries Feed Growing Nationwide Rate," press release, November 2005.

14. Center for Disease Control's National Center for Health Statistics, Preliminary Birth Data: Maternal and Infant Health, 2004.

15. M. A. Harper, "Pregnancy-Related Death and Health Care Services," *Obstetrics & Gynecology* 102, no. 2 (August 2003): 273–78.

## Chapter 10

1. Sora Song, "Too Posh to Push?" *Time,* April 19, 2004.

2. Jennifer D'Angelo, "Birth by Design: Are Celebs Too Posh to Push?" June 6, 2003, www.foxnews.com.

3. HealthGrades Quality Study, September 2005;.

4. E. Declercq et al., "Rise in 'No Indicated Risk' Primary Caesareans in the United States, 1991-2001: Cross Sectional Analysis," *British Medical Journal* 330, no. 7 (January 2005): 71–72.

5. H. P. Dietz et al., "The Effect of Childbirth on Pelvic Organ Mobility," *Obstetrics & Gynecology* 102, no. 2 (August 2003): 223–28.

6. G. M. Buchsbaum et al., "Urinary Incontinence in Nulliparous Women and Their Parous Sisters," *Obstetrics & Gynecology* 106, no. 6 (December 2005): 1253–58.

7. K. Kenton et al., "Repeat Cesarean Section and Primary Elective

Cesarean Section: Recently Trained Obstetrician-Gynecologist Practice Patterns and Opinions," *American Journal of Obstetrics & Gynecology* 192, no. 4 (April 2005): 1872–76.

8. *Ethics in Obstetrics and Gynecology* (Washington, D.C.: The American College of Obstetricians and Gynecologists, 2004), 21–25.

9. Nicette Jukelevics, "Once a Cesarean, Always a Cesarean: The Sorry State of Birth Choices in America," *Mothering,* March/April 2004.

10. M.F. Dorman et al., "Infant and Neonatal Mortality for Primary Cesarean and Vaginal Births to Women with 'No Indicated Risk.' United States, 1998-2001 Birth Cohorts," *Birth* 33, no 3 (September 2006); 175–182.

## Chapter 11

1. E. L. Ryding et al., "Psychological Impact of Emergency Cesarean Section in Comparison with Elective Cesarean Section, Instrumental and Normal Vaginal Delivery," *Journal of Psychosomatic Obstetrics and Gynecology* 19, no. 3 (September 1998): 135–44.

2. E. L. Ryding et al., "Experiences of Emergency Cesarean Section: A Phenomenological Study of 53 Women," *Birth* 25, no. 4 (December 1998): 246-51.

## Chapter 12

1. Carrie Bell, "Emme: Plus-Size Supermodel and Supermom," *American Baby,* October 2005.

2. Ayelet Waldman, "Truly, Madly, Guiltily," *The New York Times, March* 27, 2005, Style section.

3. Gilbert J. Grant, *Enjoy Your Labor: A New Approach to Pain Relief for Childbirth* (White Plains, NY: Russell Hastings Press, 2005), 14.

ALDEN GEWIRTZ

# ABOUT *the* AUTHOR

**M**arisa Cohen, a former senior editor at *Glamour,* has written for several health and women's magazines, including *Elle, Self, Fitness, More,* and *Prevention.* In the summer of 2001, after the birth of her first daughter, she turned her focus to parenting topics and has contributed to *Fit Pregnancy, American Baby, Parents, Parenting,* and *Conceive.* Her interactions with the moms she meets in the playground, music classes, and preschool corridors—each of whom has a unique and riveting birth story—inspired her to delve more deeply into the topic of childbirth. Cohen lives in New York City with her husband and their two children.

## Selected Titles from Seal Press

For more than thirty years, Seal Press has published groundbreaking books. By women. For women. Visit our website at www.sealpress.com.

———

*It's a Boy: Women Writers on Raising Sons* by Andrea J. Buchanan. $14.95, 1-58005-145-6. Seal's edgy take on what it's really like to raise boys, from toddlers to teens and beyond.

———

*It's a Girl: Women Writers on Raising Daughters* edited by Andrea J. Buchanan. $14.95, 1-58005-147-2. The companion title to *It's a Boy*, this anthology describes what it's like—and why it's a unique experience—to mother girls.

———

*Confessions of a Naughty Mommy: How I Found My Lost Libido* by Heidi Raykeil. $14.95, 1-58005-157-X. The Naughty Mommy shares her bedroom woes and woo-hoos with other mamas who are rediscovering their sex lives after baby and are ready to think about it, talk about it, and DO it.

———

*The Truth Behind the Mommy Wars: Who Decides What Makes a Good Mother?* by Miriam Peskowitz. $15.95, 1-58005-129-4. A groundbreaking book that reveals the truth behind the "wars" between working mothers and stay-at-home moms.

———

*I Wanna Be Sedated: 30 Writers on Parenting Teenagers* edited by Faith Conlon and Gail Hudson. $15.95, 1-58005-127-8. With hilarious and heart-felt essays, this anthology will reassure any parent of a teenager that they are not alone in their desire to be comatose.

———

*Literary Mama: Reading for the Maternally Inclined* edited by Andrea J. Buchanan and Amy Hudock. $14.95, 1-58005-158-8. From the best of literarymama.com, this collection of personal writing includes creative nonfiction, fiction, and poetry.